CHRIST-CENTERED LIVING FOR TEEN GUYS

W9-DCH-298

RADICAL RECKLESS AND RELENTLESS

30 DEVOTIONS

FAMILY
Christian Stores

The quoted ideas expressed in this book (but not scripture verses) are not, in all cases, exact quotations, as some have been edited for clarity and brevity. In all cases, the author has attempted to maintain the speaker's original intent. In some cases, quoted material for this book was obtained from secondary sources, primarily print media. While every effort was made to ensure the accuracy of these sources, the accuracy cannot be guaranteed. For additions, deletions, corrections or clarifications in future editions of this text, please write FAMILY CHRISTIAN STORES.

Scripture quotations are taken from:

The Holy Bible, King James Version (KJV)

The Holy Bible, New International Version (NIV) Copyright © 1973, 1978, 1984, by International Bible Society. Used by permission of Zondervan Publishing House. All rights reserved.

The Holy Bible, New King James Version (NKJV) Copyright © 1982 by Thomas Nelson, Inc. Used by permission.

Holy Bible, New Living Translation, (NLT) copyright © 1996. Used by permission of Tyndale House Publishers, Inc., Wheaton, Illinois 60189. All rights reserved.

The Message (MSG)- This edition issued by contractual arrangement with NavPress, a division of The Navigators, U.S.A. Originally published by NavPress in English as THE MESSAGE: The Bible in Contemporary Language copyright 2002-2003 by Eugene Peterson. All rights reserved.

New Century Version®. (NCV) Copyright © 1987, 1988, 1991 by Word Publishing, a division of Thomas Nelson, Inc. All rights reserved. Used by permission.

The New American Standard Bible®, (NASB) Copyright © 1960, 1962, 1963, 1968, 1971, 1972, 1973, 1975, 1977, 1995 by The Lockman Foundation. Used by permission.

The Holman Christian Standard Bible™ (HCSB) Copyright © 1999, 2000, 2001 by Holman Bible Publishers. Used by permission.

Cover Design Kim Russell / Wahoo Designs

Page Layout by Bart Dawson

ISBN 978-1-58334-016-5

Printed in the United States of America

RADICAL RECKLESS AND RELENTLESS

30 DEVOTIONS

Table of Contents

Introduction

Radical, reckless, relentless: these are three words that can—and should—define your relationship with Jesus.

Have you spent much time thinking about your relationship with God's Son? As you contemplate the nature of that relationship—and precisely what Christ means to you—here are a few things to consider:

1. You will have a relationship with Jesus; the only question is the nature of that relationship. The burning question is whether that relationship will be one that seeks to place Him first or one that attempts to relegate Him to a position of lesser importance.

2. Your relationship with Jesus is ongoing; it unfolds day by day, and it offers countless opportunities to grow closer to Him . . . or not. As each new day unfolds, you are confronted with a wide range of decisions: how you will behave, where you will direct your thoughts, with whom you will associate, and what you will choose to worship. These choices, along with many others, are yours and yours alone. How you choose determines how your relationship with Jesus will unfold.

3. Jesus doesn't call you to be a run-of-the-mill, lukewarm believer. He invites you to form a radical, life-

changing relationship with Him. When you accept Christ's invitation—when you allow Him to transform your life now and forever—you will be a different man.

4. Once you decide to follow Christ completely and without reservation, you will gain the courage to become reckless in pursuit of His goals. You will, when necessary, take risks for Him as you seek to follow in His footsteps and do the work of His kingdom.

5. Your decision to seek a deeper relationship with Christ will not remove all problems from your life; to the contrary, it will bring about a series of personal crises as you constantly seek to say "yes" to God, although the world encourages you to do otherwise. Your responsibility—a responsibility that you must take very seriously—is to follow Christ and serve Him relentlessly, even when you're tempted to give in or give up.

During the next 30 days, you'll be challenged to become a more radical, a more reckless, and a more relentless Christian. Every day provides opportunities to put Jesus where He belongs: at the center of your life. When you do so, you will worship Him not just with words, but with deeds. You will take risks for Him, and you will summon the strength to persevere in your faith.

So take the ideas in this book to heart, and apply them to your life. When you do, you'll be doing yourself—and your loved ones—a big favor today, tomorrow, and every day of your life.

Part 1

RADICAL

Chapter 1

Are You Radical?

Your old life is dead. Your new life, which is your real life—
even though invisible to spectators—is with Christ in God.
He is your life.

Colossians 3:3 MSG

THOUGHT OF THE DAY

Unless you're a radically different person because
of your relationship with Jesus,
your faith isn't what it could be . . . or should be.

When you stop to think about it, Jesus was radical . . . very radical. He arrived here on earth in a radical way, He performed radical deeds, He made radical claims, and He asked His followers to make radical changes in their lives.

Are you ready to have a radical relationship with that radical Jesus? Or are you satisfied to be a part-time Christian who keeps Jesus at a "safe" distance? If you're determined to be a part-timer, then the idea of a radical Jesus isn't too pleasant to think about. But, if you sincerely seek to become something more than a casual Christian, if you're really searching for a life-altering relationship with the Man from Galilee, then the idea of following a radical Jesus isn't really a sacrifice at all—it's a priceless blessing and a glorious opportunity.

Are you a radically different person because of your decision to form a personal relationship with Jesus? Has Jesus made a BIG difference in your life, or are you basically the same guy you were before you invited Him into your heart? The answers to these questions will determine the quality and the direction of your life.

If you're still doing all the same things you did before you became a Christian, it may be time to take an honest look at the current condition of your faith. Why? Because Jesus doesn't want you to be a one-day-a-week Christian or a follow-the-crowd kind of guy—far from it. Jesus wants you to be a "new creation" through Him. And that's exactly what you should want for yourself, too.

So today, as you begin a 30-day journey toward a deeper relationship with God and His only begotten Son, here's the million-dollar question: Are you determined to build a more meaningful relationship with Jesus? If so, you may be certain of this fact: He's standing at the door of your heart, patiently waiting to form a radical, life-altering relationship with you.

Christ's work of making new men
is not mere improvement,
but transformation.

—

C. S. Lewis

MORE IDEAS ABOUT FAITH
THAT TRANSFORMS

When the Spirit illuminates the heart, then a part of the man sees which never saw before; a part of him knows which never knew before . . . .

Oswald Chambers

God wants to revolutionize our lives—by showing us how knowing Him can be the most powerful force to help us become all we want to be.

Bill Hybels

The essence of salvation is an about-face from self-centeredness to God-centeredness.

Henry Blackaby

When we become Christians, we are not remodeled, nor are we added to—we are transformed.

John MacArthur

No man is ever the same after God has laid His hand upon him.

A. W. Tozer

If God can fashion the mountains, if God can keep the sun in its orbit, if God can split a sea and dry the ground beneath it so an entire nation can cross, do you doubt that he can transform your character?

Bill Hybels

God wants to change our lives—and He will, as we open our hearts to Him.

Billy Graham

God is not running an antique shop! He is making all things new!

Vance Havner

After ten thousand insults, he still loves you as infinitely as ever.

C. H. Spurgeon

Believe and do what God says. The life-changing consequences will be limitless, and the results will be confidence and peace of mind.

Franklin Graham

MORE FROM GOD'S WORD

Therefore if anyone is in Christ, he is a new creature; the old things passed away; behold, new things have come.

2 Corinthians 5:17 HCSB

Repent therefore and be converted, that your sins may be blotted out, so that times of refreshing may come from the presence of the Lord, and that He may send Jesus Christ, who was preached to you before.

Acts 3:19-20 NKJV

When we were baptized, we were buried with Christ and shared his death. So, just as Christ was raised from the dead by the wonderful power of the Father, we also can live a new life.

Romans 6:4 NCV

I am the door. If anyone enters by Me, he will be saved.

John 10:9 NKJV

For the Son of Man has come to save that which was lost.

Matthew 18:11 NKJV

QUESTIONS TO THINK & WRITE ABOUT

Is my life radically different because of my relationship with Jesus Christ? If so, how so? If not, why not?

_____

_____

_____

_____

What circumstances or attitudes are interfering with God's plan for my life?

_____

_____

_____

_____

Am I willing to make major changes in my life if I believe that those changes will make me a better Christian and a better man?

_____

_____

_____

_____

SUMMING IT UP

Jesus made radical sacrifices for you, and now He's asking you to make radical changes for Him. Are you willing to be a radical Christian? If so, you will be blessed for your willingness to serve God and to walk faithfully and closely in the footsteps of His only begotten Son.

A PRAYER FOR TODAY

Dear Lord, thank You for the gift of Your Son Jesus, my personal Savior. I will be His faithful, obedient servant, and I will make radical changes in my life for Him. I offer my life to You, Lord, so that I might live with passion and with purpose. And I will praise You for Your Son and for Your everlasting love. Amen

Chapter 2

Really Following Jesus

If anyone serves Me, let him follow Me;
and where I am, there My servant will be also.
If anyone serves Me, him My Father will honor.

John 12:26 NKJV

THOUGHT OF THE DAY

It takes a radical commitment—and significant sacrifices—to really follow Jesus. And it's worth it.

J esus walks with you. Are you really walking with Him? And has He made a radical difference in your life—an unmistakable difference in the way you think and the way you behave? Hopefully, you can answer the questions with a resounding yes. After all, Jesus loved you so much that He endured unspeakable humiliation and suffering. And He did it for you.

How will you respond to Christ's sacrifice? Will you take up His cross and follow Him (Luke 9:23), or will you choose another path? When you place your hopes squarely at the foot of the cross, when you place Jesus squarely at the center of your life, you will become a radical disciple, and that's precisely the kind of disciple Christ wants you to be.

Today provides yet another glorious opportunity to place yourself in the service of the One from Galilee. May you seek His will, may you trust His Word, and may you walk in His footsteps. When you do, you'll demonstrate that your acquaintance with the Master is not a passing fancy, but is, instead, the cornerstone and the touchstone of your life.

MORE IDEAS ABOUT FOLLOWING JESUS

Our responsibility is to feed from Him, to stay close to Him, to follow Him—because sheep easily go astray—so that we eternally experience the protection and companionship of our Great Shepherd the Lord Jesus Christ.

Franklin Graham

Christ is not valued at all unless He is valued above all.

St. Augustine

Imagine the spiritual strength the disciples drew from walking hundreds of miles with Jesus . . . (3 John 4).

Jim Maxwell

A believer comes to Christ; a disciple follows after Him.

Vance Havner

The heaviest end of the cross lies ever on His shoulders. If He bids us carry a burden, He carries it also.

C. H. Spurgeon

Being a Christian is more than just an instantaneous conversion; it is like a daily process whereby you grow to be more and more like Christ.

Billy Graham

MORE FROM GOD'S WORD

Then he told them what they could expect for themselves: "Anyone who intends to come with me has to let me lead."

Luke 9:23 MSG

I've laid down a pattern for you. What I've done, you do.

John 13:15 MSG

No one can serve two masters. Either he will hate the one and love the other, or he will be devoted to the one and despise the other.

Matthew 6:24 NIV

Whoever is not willing to carry the cross and follow me is not worthy of me. Those who try to hold on to their lives will give up true life. Those who give up their lives for me will hold on to true life.

Matthew 10:38-39 NCV

If anyone would come after me, he must deny himself and take up his cross and follow me.

Mark 8:34 NIV

QUESTIONS TO THINK & WRITE ABOUT

Do I really believe that my relationship with Jesus should be one of servant and Master? And am I behaving like His servant?

_____

_____

_____

_____

Am I attempting to follow in Christ's footsteps, despite my imperfections?

_____

_____

_____

_____

Do I sense a joyful abundance that is mine when I follow Christ?

_____

_____

_____

_____

SUMMING IT UP

Think about your relationship with Jesus: what it is,
and what it should be. If you sincerely wish
to follow in Christ's footsteps, welcome Him into
your heart, obey His commandments,
and share His never-ending love.

A PRAYER FOR TODAY

Dear Lord, You sent Jesus to save the world
and to save me. I thank You for Jesus,
and I will do my best to follow Him, today and forever.
Amen

Chapter 3

Striving for Righteousness by Putting God First

Walk in a manner worthy of the God who calls you into His own kingdom and glory.

1 Thessalonians 2:12 NASB

THOUGHT OF THE DAY

If you really want to follow Jesus, you must walk as He walked—you must try to lead a righteous life, despite your imperfections.

Are you determined to be an example of godly behavior to your family, to your friends, and to your community? If so, you've got to obey God's commandments. There are no shortcuts and no loopholes—to be a faithful Christian, you must be an obedient Christian.

So, when you're faced with a difficult choice or a powerful temptation, seek God's counsel and trust the counsel He gives. Invite God into your heart and live according to His commandments. When you do, you will be blessed today, tomorrow, and forever.

God has given you a guidebook for righteous living called the Holy Bible. It contains thorough instructions which, if followed, lead to fulfillment and salvation. But, if you choose to ignore God's commandments, the results are as predictable as they are tragic.

So here's a surefire formula for a happy, abundant life: live righteously. And for further instructions, read the manual.

Trusting God is the bottom line of Christian righteousness.

—

R. C. Sproul

MORE IDEAS ABOUT A LIFE
OF RIGHTEOUSNESS

Sanctify yourself and you will sanctify society.

St. Francis of Assisi

A man who lives right, and is right, has more power in his silence than another has by his words.

Phillips Brooks

We must appropriate the tender mercy of God every day after conversion, or problems quickly develop. We need his grace daily in order to live a righteous life.

Jim Cymbala

If we don't hunger and thirst after righteousness, we'll become anemic and feel miserable in our Christian experience.

Franklin Graham

Simplicity reaches out after God; purity discovers and enjoys him.

Thomas à Kempis

MORE FROM GOD'S WORD

For the eyes of the Lord are on the righteous, and His ears are open to their prayers; but the face of the Lord is against those who do evil.

1 Peter 3:12 NKJV

Walk in a manner worthy of the God who calls you into His own kingdom and glory.

1 Thessalonians 2:12 NASB

Discipline yourself for the purpose of godliness.

1 Timothy 4:7 NASB

Run away from infantile indulgence. Run after mature righteousness—faith, love, peace—joining those who are in honest and serious prayer before God.

2 Timothy 2:22 MSG

And you shall do what is right and good in the sight of the Lord, that it may be well with you.

Deuteronomy 6:18 NKJV

QUESTIONS TO THINK & WRITE ABOUT

Do I study God's Word each day and strive to understand God's teachings?

_____

_____

_____

Will I seek to live in accordance with Biblical teachings?

_____

_____

_____

Will I, to the best of my abilities, surround myself with like-minded believers who seek to obey God's Word?

_____

_____

_____

Will I assiduously avoid people and places that might tempt me to disobey God's commandments?

_____

_____

_____

SUMMING IT UP

When it comes to doing the right thing, don't put it off.
If you're not willing to do the right thing today,
why should you (or anybody else, for that matter)
expect you to change tomorrow?

A PRAYER FOR TODAY

Lord, Your laws are perfect; let me live by
those laws. And, let my life be a testimony to
the power of righteousness and to the wisdom
of Your commandments.
Amen

Chapter 4

Just Who Are You Really Trying to Please?

*For am I now trying to win the favor of people, or God?
Or am I striving to please people? If I were still trying to
please people, I would not be a slave of Christ.*

Galatians 1:10 HCSB

THOUGHT OF THE DAY

If you are burdened with a "people-pleasing" personality,
you may be tempted to stray from your faith. In truth, you
can't please all of the people all of the time, nor should
you attempt to. So you should focus on pleasing God.

If you're like most people, you try to be popular—but don't try too hard. Why? Because popularity is highly overrated. Your eagerness to please others should never overshadow your eagerness to please God. In every aspect of your life, pleasing your Heavenly Father should come first.

Would you like a time-tested formula for successful living? Here is a formula that is proven and true: Seek God's approval first and other people's approval later. Does this sound too simple? Perhaps it is simple, but it is also the only way to reap the marvelous riches that God has in store for you.

So, if you'd like a time-tested formula for achieving radical, life-altering success; here is a formula that is proven and true: Seek God's approval in every aspect of your life. Does this sound too simple? Perhaps it is simple, but it is also the only way to reap the marvelous riches that God has in store for you.

Those who follow the crowd usually get lost in it.

—

Rick Warren

MORE IDEAS ABOUT PLEASING GOD

Great tranquility has he who cares neither for praise nor criticism.

Thomas á Kempis

Pride opens the door to every other sin, for once we are more concerned with our reputation than our character, there is no end to the things we will do just to make ourselves "look good" before others.

Warren Wiersbe

If you try to be everything to everybody, you will end up being nothing to anybody.

Vance Havner

Fashion is an enduring testimony to the fact that we live quite consciously before the eyes of others.

John Eldredge

You should forget about trying to be popular with everybody and start trying to be popular with God Almighty.

Sam Jones

Applause is the spur of noble minds, the end and aim of weak ones.

Charles Caleb Colton

MORE FROM GOD'S WORD

Do not be misled: "Bad company corrupts good character."

1 Corinthians 15:33 NIV

Don't become partners with those who reject God. How can you make a partnership out of right and wrong? That's not partnership; that's war. Is light best friends with dark?

2 Corinthians 6:14 MSG

Friend, don't go along with evil. Model the good. The person who does good does God's work. The person who does evil falsifies God, doesn't know the first thing about God.

3 John 1:11 MSG

We must obey God rather than men.

Acts 5:29 HCSB

My son, if sinners entice you, don't be persuaded.

Proverbs 1:10 HCSB

QUESTIONS TO THINK & WRITE ABOUT

Do I actively seek out wise friends who help me make right choices?

_____

_____

_____

_____

Do I understand that being obedient to God means that I cannot always please other people?

_____

_____

_____

_____

Do I understand the importance of pleasing God first?

_____

_____

_____

_____

SUMMING IT UP

A thoughtful Christian doesn't follow the crowd . . .
a thoughtful Christian follows Jesus.

A PRAYER FOR TODAY

Dear Lord, today I will worry less about pleasing other people and more about pleasing You. I will stand up for my beliefs, and I will honor You with my thoughts, my actions, and my prayers. And I will worship You, Father, with thanksgiving in my heart, this day and forever.
Amen

Chapter 5

Are You Listening to Your Conscience, or Have You Hit the Mute Button?

So I strive always to keep my conscience clear before God and man.

Acts 24:16 NIV

THOUGHT OF THE DAY

God gave you a conscience for a very good reason:
to use it. And if you desire to be a radical,
fully involved disciple, you must learn to trust
your conscience and use it often.

When you're about to do something that you know is wrong, a little voice inside your head has a way of speaking up. That voice, of course, is your conscience: an early-warning system designed to keep you out of trouble. If you listen to that voice, you'll be okay; if you ignore it, you're asking for headaches or heartbreaks, or both.

Few things in life will torment you more than a guilty conscience. Thankfully, the reverse is also true: a clear conscience is a lasting reward that becomes yours when you know that you've done the right thing.

Whenever you're about to make an important decision, you should listen carefully to the quiet voice inside. Sometimes, of course, it's tempting to do otherwise. From time to time you'll be tempted to abandon your better judgment by ignoring your conscience. But remember: a conscience is a terrible thing to waste. So instead of ignoring that quiet little voice, pay careful attention to it. If you do, your conscience will lead you in the right direction—in fact, it's trying to lead you right now. So listen . . . and learn.

MORE IDEAS ABOUT KEEPING
YOUR CONSCIENCE CLEAR

He that loses his conscience has nothing left that is worth keeping.

Izaak Walton

Most of us follow our conscience as we follow a wheelbarrow. We push it in front of us in the direction we want to go.

Billy Graham

God considers a pure conscience a very valuable thing—one that keeps our faith on a steady course.

Charles Stanley

A good conscience is a continual feast.

Francis Bacon

The voice of the subconscious argues with you, tries to convince you; but the inner voice of God does not argue; it does not try to convince you. It just speaks, and it is self-authenticating.

E. Stanley Jones

One's conscience can only be satisfied when God is satisfied.

C. H. Spurgeon

MORE FROM GOD'S WORD

If then you were raised with Christ, seek those things which are above, where Christ is, sitting at the right hand of God. Set your mind on things above, not on things on the earth.

Colossians 3:1-2 NKJV

Let us come near to God with a sincere heart and a sure faith, because we have been made free from a guilty conscience, and our bodies have been washed with pure water.

Hebrews 10:22 NCV

I will maintain my righteousness and never let go of it; my conscience will not reproach me as long as I live.

Job 27:6 NIV

For indeed, the kingdom of God is within you.

Luke 17:21 NKJV

Create in me a pure heart, O God, and renew a steadfast spirit within me.

Psalm 51:10 NIV

QUESTIONS TO THINK & WRITE ABOUT

Do I understand the value of a clear conscience?

_____

_____

_____

_____

Do I believe that it is important that I attune my thoughts to God's will for my life?

_____

_____

_____

_____

When I prepare to make an important decision, do I listen to my conscience very carefully?

_____

_____

_____

_____

SUMMING IT UP

The more important the decision . . . the more carefully
you should listen to your conscience.

———◆◆◆◆———

A PRAYER FOR TODAY

Lord, You have given me a conscience that tells me
right from wrong. Let me listen to that quiet voice
so that I might do Your will and follow
Your Word today and every day.
Amen

Chapter 6

If You Want to Be Radically Obedient, You've Got to Answer God's Call

Thus Noah did; according to all that God commanded him, so he did.

Genesis 6:22 NKJV

THOUGHT OF THE DAY

Radical discipleship requires radical obedience.

The story of Noah's ark is one of the most familiar in the Old Testament. And when you think about it, Noah was a radical believer. Very radical. After all, when he answered God's call and began building the ark, there was not a cloud in the sky. So the naysayers had their fun, and the mockers scoffed. But Noah kept building. Why? Because God told him to. And when God calls us, we, like Noah, should answer that call with determination and faith, no matter the consequences.

God is calling you to follow a specific path that He has chosen for your life. And it is vitally important that you heed that call. Otherwise, your talents and opportunities may go unused.

God has important work for you to do—work that no one else on earth can accomplish but you. The Creator has placed you in a particular location, amid particular people, with unique opportunities to serve. And He has given you all the tools you need to succeed. So listen for His voice, watch for His signs, and prepare yourself for the call that is sure to come.

Obedience is the
outward expression
of your love of God.

—

Henry Blackaby

MORE IDEAS ABOUT OBEDIENCE TO GOD

You cannot possibly imagine all that God has in store for you when you trust him.

Henry Blackaby

Christ reigns in his church as shepherd-king. He has supremacy, but it is the superiority of a wise and tender shepherd over his needy and loving flock. He commands and receives obedience, but it is willing obedience of well-cared-for-sheep, offered joyfully to their beloved Shepherd, whose voice they know so well. He rules by the force of love and the energy of goodness.

C. H. Spurgeon

When you suffer and lose, that does not mean you are being disobedient to God. In fact, it might mean you're right in the center of His will. The path of obedience is often marked by times of suffering and loss.

Charles Swindoll

Only he who believes is obedient. Only he who is obedient believes.

Dietrich Bonhoeffer

Trials and sufferings teach us to obey the Lord by faith, and we soon learn that obedience pays off in joyful ways.

Bill Bright

Obedience is the road to freedom, humility the road to pleasure, unity the road to personality.

C. S. Lewis

You can't step in front of God and not get in trouble. When He says, "Go three steps," don't go four.

Charles Stanley

Let your fellowship with the Father and with the Lord Jesus Christ have as its one aim and object a life of quiet, determined, unquestioning obedience.

Andrew Murray

True faith commits us to obedience.

A. W. Tozer

The strength and happiness of a man consists in finding out the way in which God is going, and going that way too.

Henry Ward Beecher

MORE FROM GOD'S WORD

Those who obey his commands live in him, and he in them. And this is how we know that he lives in us: We know it by the Spirit he gave us.

1 John 3:24 NIV

You shall walk after the Lord your God and fear Him, and keep His commandments and obey His voice, and you shall serve Him and hold fast to Him.

Deuteronomy 13:4 NKJV

When all has been heard, the conclusion of the matter is: fear God and keep His commands.

Ecclesiastes 12:13 HCSB

If they obey and serve him, they will spend the rest of their days in prosperity and their years in contentment.

Job 36:11 NIV

For it is not those who hear the law who are righteous in God's sight, but it is those who obey the law who will be declared righteous.

Romans 2:13 NIV

QUESTIONS TO THINK & WRITE ABOUT

Am I willing to study God's Word seriously and consistently?

_____

_____

_____

_____

Will I strive to obey God's commandments?

_____

_____

_____

_____

Will I associate with fellow believers who, by their words and actions, encourage me to obey God?

_____

_____

_____

_____

SUMMING IT UP

When you are obedient to God, you are secure;
when you are not, you are not.

A PRAYER FOR TODAY

Lord, when it's difficult being a Christian,
give me the courage and the wisdom to stand up
for my faith. Christ made the ultimate sacrifice for me;
let me now stand up for Him!
Amen

Chapter 7

Are You Just a Little Too Distracted with the World?

Do you not know that friendship with the world is hostility toward God? So whoever wants to be the world's friend becomes God's enemy.

James 4:4 HCSB

THOUGHT OF THE DAY

The world is designed to distract you—and distance you—from your faith. So you must guard yourself against these distractions . . . or face the consequences.

W e live in the world, but we should not worship it—yet at every turn, or so it seems, we are tempted to do otherwise. As Warren Wiersbe correctly observed, "Because the world is deceptive, it is dangerous."

Are you overly concerned with the stuff that money can buy? If so, here's a word of warning: your love for material possessions is getting in the way of your relationship with God.

Up on the stage of life, material possessions should play a rather small role. Of course, we all need the basic necessities like food, clothing, and a place to live. But once we've met those needs, the piling up of possessions creates more problems than it solves. Our real riches, of course, are not of this world. We're never really rich until we are rich in spirit.

Our society is in love with money and the things that money can buy. God is not. God cares about people, not possessions, and so must we. We must, to the best of our abilities, love our neighbors as ourselves, and we must, to the best of our abilities, resist the mighty temptation to place possessions ahead of people.

Money, in and of itself, is not evil; worshipping money is. So today, as you seek better ways to know your Creator, remember that God is almighty, but the dollar is not.

MORE IDEAS ABOUT THE DANGERS OF BECOMING TOO WORLDLY

The world's sewage system threatens to contaminate the stream of Christian thought. Is the world shaping your mind, or is Christ?

Billy Graham

The true Christian, though he is in revolt against the world's efforts to brainwash him, is no mere rebel for rebellion's sake. He dissents from the world because he knows that it cannot make good on its promises.

A. W. Tozer

The socially prescribed affluent, middle-class lifestyle has become so normative in our churches that we discern little conflict between it and the Christian lifestyle prescribed in the New Testament.

Tony Campolo

The Lord Jesus Christ is still praying for us. He wants us to be in the world but not of it.

Charles Stanley

Our joy ends where love of the world begins.

C. H. Spurgeon

MORE FROM GOD'S WORD

Let no one deceive himself. If anyone among you seems to be wise in this age, let him become a fool that he may become wise. For the wisdom of this world is foolishness with God. For it is written, "He catches the wise in their own craftiness."

1 Corinthians 3:18–19 NKJV

Do not love the world or the things in the world. If you love the world, the love of the Father is not in you.

1 John 2:15 NCV

For whatever is born of God overcomes the world. And this is the victory that has overcome the world—our faith.

1 John 5:4 NKJV

Religion that God our Father accepts as pure and faultless is this: to look after orphans and widows in their distress and to keep oneself from being polluted by the world.

James 1:27 NIV

If you lived on the world's terms, the world would love you as one of its own. But since I picked you to live on God's terms and no longer on the world's terms, the world is going to hate you.

John 15:19 MSG

QUESTIONS TO THINK & WRITE ABOUT

Will I focus on the world's values or God's values?

_____

_____

_____

_____

Do I allow myself to be sidetracked by the inevitable distractions and temptations of everyday life?

_____

_____

_____

_____

Do I begin each day by meditating on God's Word and God's love, or do I sleep until the last minute and then rush headlong into the day?

_____

_____

_____

_____

SUMMING IT UP

Your world is full of distractions and temptations.
Your challenge is to live in the world
but not be of the world.

————◆————

A PRAYER FOR TODAY

Lord, this world is a crazy place, and I have many
opportunities to stray from Your commandments.
Help me to obey You! Let me keep Christ
in my heart, and let me put the devil in his place:
far away from me!
Amen

Chapter 8

Radical Hopes, Radical Dreams

Live full lives, full in the fullness of God.
God can do anything, you know—far more than you could
ever imagine or guess or request in your wildest dreams!
He does it not by pushing us around but by working within us,
his Spirit deeply and gently within us.

Ephesians 3:19-20 MSG

THOUGHT OF THE DAY

When you make the radical commitment to follow Jesus
completely and without reservation,
you can dream radically large dreams.

How big are you willing to dream? Are you willing to entertain the possibility that God has big plans in store for you? Or are you convinced that your future is so dim that you'd better wear night goggles? Well here's the facts, Jack: if you're a believer in the One from Galilee, you have an incredibly bright future ahead of you . . . here on earth and in heaven. That's why you have every right to dream big.

Concentration camp survivor Corrie ten Boom observed, "Every experience God gives us, every person he brings into our lives, is the perfect preparation for the future that only he can see." These words apply to you.

It takes courage to dream big dreams. You will discover that courage when you do three things: accept the past, trust God to handle the future, and make the most of the time He has given you today.

Nothing is too difficult for God, and no dreams are too big for Him—not even yours. So start living—and dreaming—accordingly.

MORE IDEAS ABOUT YOUR DREAMS

The Christian believes in a fabulous future.

Billy Graham

Set goals so big that unless God helps you, you will be a miserable failure.

Bill Bright

To make your dream come true, you have to stay awake.

Dennis Swanberg

Great opportunities often disguise themselves in small tasks.

Rick Warren

We must be willing to give up every dream but God's dream.

Larry Crabb

You cannot out-dream God.

John Eldredge

MORE FROM GOD'S WORD

I came so they can have real and eternal life, more and better life than they ever dreamed of.

John 10:10 MSG

It is pleasant to see dreams come true, but fools will not turn from evil to attain them.

Proverbs 13:19 NLT

Where there is no vision, the people perish . . . .

Proverbs 29:18 KJV

Be of good courage, and he shall strengthen your heart, all ye that hope in the LORD.

Psalm 31:24 KJV

Now may the God of hope fill you with all joy and peace in believing, so that you may overflow with hope by the power of the Holy Spirit.

Romans 15:13 HCSB

QUESTIONS TO THINK & WRITE ABOUT

Do I place my hopes in God?

_____

_____

_____

_____

Do I prayerfully seek to understand God's plans for my life?

_____

_____

_____

_____

Do I place limitations on myself, and do I place limitations on God's power to use me for His purposes?

_____

_____

_____

_____

SUMMING IT UP

Be a dreamer: Your attitude toward the future will help create your future. So think realistically about yourself (and your situation) but focus your thoughts on hopes, not fears. When you do, you'll put the self-fulfilling prophecy to work for you.

A PRAYER FOR TODAY

Dear Lord, give me the courage to dream and the faithfulness to trust in Your perfect plan. When I am worried or weary, give me strength for today and hope for tomorrow. Keep me mindful of Your healing power, Your infinite love, and Your eternal salvation.
Amen

Chapter 9

Pleasing God

Teach me, O Lord, the way of Your statutes,
and I shall keep it to the end. Give me understanding,
and I shall keep Your law; indeed,
I shall observe it with my whole heart.

Psalm 119:33-34 NKJV

THOUGHT OF THE DAY

Every step of your life's journey is a choice . . .
and the quality of those choices determines the quality
of the journey. It's up to you (and you alone)
to make sure that your choices please God.

When God made you, He equipped you with an array of talents and abilities that are uniquely yours. It's up to you to discover those talents and to use them, but sometimes the world will encourage you to do otherwise. At times, society will attempt to cubbyhole you, to standardize you, and to make you fit into a particular, preformed mold. Perhaps God has other plans.

Sometimes, because you're an imperfect human being, you may become so wrapped up in meeting your peer's expectations that you fail to focus on God's expectations. To do so is a mistake of major proportions—don't make it. Instead, seek God's guidance as you focus your energies on becoming the person God wants you to be.

As you make plans for the day ahead, how do you intend to use the talents God has given you? Will you try to please God or people? Your primary obligation is not to please imperfect guys or girls. Your obligation is to do your best to meet the expectations of an all-knowing and perfect God. Trust Him always. Love Him always. Praise Him always. And seek to please Him. Always.

MORE IDEAS ABOUT PLEASING GOD

It is impossible to please everybody. It's not impossible to please God. So try pleasing God.

Jim Gallery

All our offerings, whether music or martyrdom, are like the intrinsically worthless present of a child, which a father values indeed, but values only for the intention.

C. S. Lewis

It is impossible to please God doing things motivated by and produced by the flesh.

Bill Bright

Your life together with other believers stands as the best confirmation that you know God.

Stanley Grenz

We learn to determine the will of God by working at it. The more we obey, the easier it is to discover what God wants us to do.

Warren Wiersbe

When we truly walk with God throughout our day, life slowly starts to fall into place.

Bill Hybels

MORE FROM GOD'S WORD

Be energetic in your life of salvation, reverent and sensitive before God. That energy is God's energy, an energy deep within you, God himself willing and working at what will give him the most pleasure.

Philippians 2:12-13 MSG

Obviously, I'm not trying to be a people pleaser! No, I am trying to please God. If I were still trying to please people, I would not be Christ's servant.

Galatians 1:10 NLT

Everything that goes into a life of pleasing God has been miraculously given to us by getting to know, personally and intimately, the One who invited us to God. The best invitation we ever received!

2 Peter 1:3 MSG

Our only goal is to please God whether we live here or there, because we must all stand before Christ to be judged.

2 Corinthians 5:9-10 NCV

If you love Me, you will keep My commandments.

John 14:15 HCSB

QUESTIONS TO THINK & WRITE ABOUT

Do I understand the importance of pleasing God first and people later, or am I sometimes too focused on pleasing people?

_____

_____

_____

_____

Do I try to associate with people who, by their actions and their words, encourage me to become a better person?

_____

_____

_____

_____

Do I understand that it's more important to be respected than to be liked?

_____

_____

_____

_____

SUMMING IT UP

You should be far more concerned with pleasing
God than with pleasing any person on earth
(including yourself).

A PRAYER FOR TODAY

Lord, You know my heart, and You're concerned
with the "inner me." Today, I will worry less about
what other people think . . . and I'll worry
more about what You think.
Amen

Chapter 10

God's Plan

You will show me the path of life; in Your presence is fullness of joy; at Your right hand are pleasures forevermore.

Psalm 16:11 NKJV

THOUGHT OF THE DAY

God has a plan for your life and He's trying to get His message through to you. Your job, simply put, is to pray for guidance and to watch for His signs.

The Bible makes it clear: God's got a plan—a whopper of a plan—and you play a vitally important role in it. But here's the catch: God won't force His plans upon you; you've got to figure things out for yourself . . . or not.

As a Christian, you should ask yourself this question: "How closely can I make my plans match God's plans?" The more closely you manage to follow the path that God intends for your life, the better.

Do you have questions or concerns about the future? Take them to God in prayer. Do you have hopes and expectations? Talk to God about your dreams. Are you carefully planning for the days and weeks ahead? Consult God as you establish your priorities. Turn every concern over to your Heavenly Father, and sincerely seek His guidance—prayerfully, earnestly, and often. Then, listen for His answers . . . and trust the answers that He gives.

Sometimes, God's plans are crystal clear, but other times, He may lead you through the wilderness before He delivers you to the Promised Land. So be patient, keep praying, and keep seeking His will for your life. When you do, you'll be amazed at the marvelous things that an all-powerful, all-knowing God can do.

God has a plan for the life
of every Christian.
Every circumstance,
every turn of destiny,
all things work together
for your good and for His glory.

—

Billy Graham

MORE IDEAS ABOUT GOD'S PLAN

It's been said that when God sends you on a journey, He will direct your path and light your way, even if it's only one step at a time. And from walking the mountains and valleys of my own life, I believe that to be true. When the Lord is with me, I can feel his presence and move out in confidence, and although I may not know my final destination, I have his assurance that I'm heading in the right direction.

Al Green

God would not have created us without a specific plan in mind.

Erwin Lutzer

It's incredible to realize that what we do each day has meaning in the big picture of God's plan.

Bill Hybels

The aim of God in history is the creation of an all-inclusive community of loving persons, with Himself included in that community as its prime sustainer and most glorious inhabitant.

Dallas Willard

God has a course mapped out for your life, and all the inadequacies in the world will not change His mind. He will be with you every step of the way. And though it may take time, He has a celebration planned for when you cross over the "Red Seas" of your life.

Charles Swindoll

I find the doing of the will of God leaves me no time for disputing about His plans.

George MacDonald

The one supreme business of life is to find God's plan for your life and live it.

E. Stanley Jones

I can't claim ever to have had even a glimpse of God. When I look back on my life, however, I see his tracks all around the places where I have been.

Glenn Tinder

The strength and happiness of a man consists in finding out the way in which God is going, and going that way too.

Henry Ward Beecher

MORE FROM GOD'S WORD

Who are those who fear the Lord? He will show them the path they should choose. They will live in prosperity, and their children will inherit the Promised Land.

Psalm 25:12-13 NLT

And we know that in all things God works for the good of those who love him, who have been called according to his purpose.

Romans 8:28 NIV

The steps of the Godly are directed by the Lord. He delights in every detail of their lives. Though they stumble, they will not fall, for the Lord holds them by the hand.

Psalm 37:23-24 NLT

It is God who works in you to will and to act according to his good purpose.

Philippians 2:13 NIV

"For I know the plans I have for you," declares the Lord, "plans to prosper you and not to harm you, plans to give you hope and a future. Then you will call upon me and come and pray to me, and I will listen to you."

Jeremiah 29:11-12 NIV

QUESTIONS TO THINK & WRITE ABOUT

Am I really seeking God's will for my life, or am I just going through the motions?

_____

_____

_____

_____

Since I believe that God has a plan for my day, do I set aside enough quiet time each morning in order to seek His will for my life?

_____

_____

_____

_____

Do I regularly ask God to reveal His plans to me, and when I pray, do I listen carefully for His response?

_____

_____

_____

_____

SUMMING IT UP

God has a wonderful plan for your life.
And the time to start looking for that plan—
and living it—is now. And remember:
Discovering God's plan begins with prayer.

A PRAYER FOR TODAY

Lord, You have plans for my life that are far more grand
than I can imagine. I will study Your Word,
pray for Your guidance, and seek Your will
so that my life might be a tribute to Your Son.
Amen

Part 2

RECKLESS

Chapter 11

Are You Just a Little Too Comfortable?

Be strong and courageous, and do the work.
Don't be afraid or discouraged, for the Lord God, my God,
is with you. He won't leave you or forsake you.

1 Chronicles 28:20 HCSB

THOUGHT OF THE DAY

It's easy to become comfortable with the status quo,
but often it's wrong. Sometimes, God wants you
to take risks for Him. And that means that you
may have to be a little reckless at times.

Risk is an inevitable fact of life. From the moment we arise in the morning until the moment we drift off to sleep at night, we face a wide array of risks, both great and small. Some risks, of course, should be avoided at all costs—these include risky behaviors that drive us farther and farther away from God's will for our lives. Yet other risks—the kinds of risks that we must take in order to expand our horizons and expand our faith—should be accepted as the inevitable price we must pay for living full and productive lives.

Have you planted yourself firmly inside your own comfort zone? If so, it's time to reconsider the direction and scope of your activities. God has big plans for you, but those plans will most likely require you to expand your comfort zone—or leave it altogether.

Today, ask God for the courage to step beyond the boundaries of your doubts. Ask Him to guide you to a place where you can realize your full potential—a place where you are freed from the fear of failure. Ask Him to do His part, and promise Him that you will do your part. Don't ask Him to lead you to a "safe" place; ask Him to lead you to the "right" place . . . and remember: those two places are seldom the same.

There comes a time when
we simply have to face
the challenges in our lives
and stop backing down.

—

John Eldredge

MORE IDEAS ABOUT MOVING OUTSIDE YOUR COMFORT ZONE

The really committed leave the safety of the harbor, accept the risk of the open seas of faith, and set their compasses for the place of total devotion to God and whatever life adventures He plans for them.

Bill Hybels

You never know how much you really believe anything until its truth or falsehood becomes a matter of life and death to you. It is easy to say you believe a rope to be strong and sound as long as you are merely using it to cord a box. But suppose you had to hang by that rope over a precipice. Wouldn't you then first discover how much you really trusted it? Only a real risk tests the reality of a belief.

C. S. Lewis

When I am secure in Christ, I can afford to take a risk in my life. Only the insecure cannot afford to risk failure. The secure can be honest about themselves; they can admit failure; they are able to seek help and try again. They can change.

John Maxwell

If we are intended for great ends, we are called to great hazards.

John Henry Cardinal Newman

We have a God who wants us to take risks, and we are accountable for the risks we don't take!

R. Paul Stevens

Believe and do what God says. The life-changing consequences will be limitless, and the results will be confidence and peace of mind.

Franklin Graham

Beware of cut-and-dried theologies that reduce the ways of God to a manageable formula that keeps life safe. God often does the unexplainable just to keep us on our toes— and also on our knees.

Warren Wiersbe

Bible hope is confidence in the future.

Warren Wiersbe

Do not let Satan deceive you into being afraid of God's plans for your life.

R. A. Torrey

MORE FROM GOD'S WORD

In all the work you are doing, work the best you can. Work as if you were doing it for the Lord, not for people.

Colossians 3:23 NCV

He did it with all his heart. So he prospered.

2 Chronicles 31:21 NKJV

Do not lack diligence; be fervent in spirit; serve the Lord.

Romans 12:11 HCSB

Do your work with enthusiasm. Work as if you were serving the Lord, not as if you were serving only men and women.

Ephesians 6:7 NCV

The thief's purpose is to steal and kill and destroy. My purpose is to give life in all its fullness.

John 10:10 NLT

QUESTIONS TO THINK & WRITE ABOUT

Will I seek to live a life that stretches me beyond my comfort zone?

_____

_____

_____

_____

Do I surround myself with people who share my passions and my sense of purpose?

_____

_____

_____

_____

Am I willing to risk it all in order to follow God's will for my life, even if it means taking risks?

_____

_____

_____

_____

SUMMING IT UP

It takes courage to step outside your comfort zone.
And it takes determination to follow your dreams in
a world where pessimism sometimes seems to be woven
into the very fabric of society. Your challenge is to
believe in yourself, to trust God, and to follow
God's lead, even if He leads you outside
your comfort zone.

A PRAYER FOR TODAY

Heavenly Father, I want to be totally committed to
Your kingdom's work. Sometimes that will involve risk.
Help me know when I should take sensible risks
in order to accomplish Your will for my life.
Amen

Chapter 12

The Ultimate Risk-Reward: Giving Your Life to God's Son

Therefore if anyone is in Christ, he is a new creature; the old things passed away; behold, new things have come.

2 Corinthians 5:17 HCSB

THOUGHT OF THE DAY

When you allow Christ to rule your heart, you take a risk (by giving up many things that the world values) in order to earn a priceless reward (by earning peace here on earth and eternal life in heaven).

Giving your heart to Christ means that you're willing to take a risk. After all, when you commit your mind, body, and soul to God, you know that you'll be giving up many of the things that the world holds dear. But with that risk comes an unimaginable rewards: the gift of eternal life, the peace that passes all understanding, and the knowledge that you've chosen to follow in the footsteps of God's Son.

Have you invited God's Son into your heart? And has your relationship with Jesus transformed you into an extremely different person? Hopefully so. Otherwise, you're missing out on the joy and abundance that can be yours through Christ.

Think, for a moment, about the "old" you, the person you were before you accepted Christ. Now, think about the "new" you, the person you've become since then. Is there a difference between the "old" version of you and the "new-and-improved" version? There should be! And that difference should be evident to you, to your family, and to your friends.

When you invited Christ to reign over your heart, you become a radically new creation. This day offers yet another opportunity to behave yourself like that new person. When you do, God will guide your steps and bless your endeavors . . . forever.

Are you willing to make radical changes for Jesus? If so, you may be certain of this fact: He's standing at the door of your heart, patiently waiting to form an extreme, life-altering relationship with you.

MORE IDEAS ABOUT YOUR TRANSFORMATION

Christ is the only way to God, but there are as many ways to Christ as there are people who come to him.

Os Guinness

God is not running an antique shop! He is making all things new!

Vance Havner

True conversion involves a turning toward God, others, and creation, and in this manner it is a turning even toward yourself.

Stanley Grenz

We had better quickly discover whether we have mere religion or a real experience with Jesus, whether we have outward observance of religious forms or hearts that beat in tune with God.

Jim Cymbala

MORE FROM GOD'S WORD

Whoever believes that Jesus is the Christ is born of God, and whoever loves the Father loves the child born of Him.

1 John 5:1 NASB

If anyone belongs to Christ, there is a new creation. The old things have gone; everything is made new!

2 Corinthians 5:17 NCV

Your old life is dead. Your new life, which is your real life— even though invisible to spectators—is with Christ in God. He is your life.

Colossians 3:3 MSG

You were taught to leave your old self—to stop living the evil way you lived before. That old self becomes worse, because people are fooled by the evil things they want to do. But you were taught to be made new in your hearts, to become a new person. That new person is made to be like God—made to be truly good and holy.

Ephesians 4:22–24 NCV

Jesus answered and said to him, "Truly, truly, I say to you, unless one is born again he cannot see the kingdom of God."

John 3:3 NASB

QUESTIONS TO THINK & WRITE ABOUT

Do I believe that God offers me the gift of eternal life through the sacrifice of His Son Jesus?

_____

_____

_____

_____

Am I confident about my relationship with Jesus, and do I believe that I will spend eternity with Him in heaven?

_____

_____

_____

_____

Does God's promise of salvation give me comfort and peace?

_____

_____

_____

_____

SUMMING IT UP

A true conversion experience results in a life
transformed by Christ and a commitment
to following in His footsteps.

A PRAYER FOR TODAY

Lord, when I accepted Jesus as my personal Savior,
You changed me forever and made me whole.
Let me share Your Son's message with my friends,
with my family, and with the world. You are
a God of love, redemption, conversion, and salvation.
I will praise You today and forever.
Amen

Chapter 13

Taking Some Risks in Order to Serve

So prepare your minds for service and have self-control.
All your hope should be for the gift of grace that will be
yours when Jesus Christ is shown to you.

1 Peter 1:13 NCV

THOUGHT OF THE DAY

By climbing up on the roof, the men took a risk in order
to serve their paralyzed friend. We, too, should be willing
to take risks in order to serve our neighbors.

Sometimes, if you're determined to do what needs to be done, you must take risks. And so it was with the friends who are described in the 5th chapter of Luke. These men intended to deliver their paralyzed friend to Jesus so that the Master might heal their companion. But because Jesus was inside a crowded building, the friends could not reach Him. So what did they do? They took a risk by climbing atop the building and lowering their comrade through an opening in the roof. And, of course, their risk paid off when their friend was healed by the Master's touch.

Sometimes you, like the men in Luke 5, will be called to take risks in the service of others. And if you're a radical believer, you'll summon the courage to do the right thing.

If you genuinely want to make choices that are pleasing to God, you must ask yourself this question: "How does God want me to serve others?"

Whatever your age, wherever you happen to be, you may be certain of this: service to others is an integral part of God's plan for your life.

Every single day of your life, including this one, God will give you opportunities to serve Him by serving other people. Welcome those opportunities with open arms. They are God's gift to you, His way of allowing you to achieve greatness in His kingdom.

Service is the pathway to
real significance.

—

Rick Warren

MORE IDEAS ABOUT SERVING OTHERS

No life can surpass that of a man who quietly continues to serve God in the place where providence has placed him.

C. H. Spurgeon

Before the judgment seat of Christ, my service will not be judged by how much I have done but by how much of me there is in it.

A. W. Tozer

When you're enjoying the fulfillment and fellowship that inevitably accompanies authentic service, ministry is a joy. Instead of exhausting you, it energizes you; instead of burnout, you experience blessing.

Bill Hybels

Make it a rule, and pray to God to help you to keep it, never, if possible, to lie down at night without being able to say: "I have made one human being at least a little wiser, or a little happier, or at least a little better this day."

Charles Kingsley

In Jesus, the service of God and the service of the least of the brethren were one.

Dietrich Bonhoeffer

You can judge how far you have risen in the scale of life by asking one question: How wisely and how deeply do I care? To be Christianized is to be sensitized. Christians are people who care.

E. Stanley Jones

In God's family, there is to be one great body of people: servants. In fact, that's the way to the top in his kingdom.

Charles Swindoll

If doing a good act in public will excite others to do more good, then "Let your Light shine to all." Miss no opportunity to do good.

John Wesley

God does not do anything with us, only through us.

Oswald Chambers

Opportunities for service abound, and you will be surprised that when you seek God's direction, a place of suitable service will emerge where you can express your love through service.

Charles Stanley

MORE FROM GOD'S WORD

There are different kinds of gifts, but they are all from the same Spirit. There are different ways to serve but the same Lord to serve.

1 Corinthians 12:4–5 NCV

If they serve Him obediently, they will end their days in prosperity and their years in happiness.

Job 36:11 HCSB

Whoever serves me must follow me. Then my servant will be with me everywhere I am. My Father will honor anyone who serves me.

John 12:26 NCV

On one of those days while He was teaching, Pharisees and teachers of the law were sitting there who had come from every village of Galilee and Judea, and also from Jerusalem. And the Lord's power to heal was in Him. Just then some men came, carrying on a stretcher a man who was paralyzed. They tried to bring him in and set him down before Him. Since they could not find a way to bring him in because of the crowd, they went up on the roof and lowered him on the stretcher through the roof tiles into the middle of the crowd before Jesus. Seeing their faith He said, "Friend, your sins are forgiven you."

Luke 5:17-20 HCSB

QUESTIONS TO THINK & WRITE ABOUT

Am I willing to serve God by being a faithful steward of
the talents He has entrusted to my care?

_____

_____

_____

_____

Do I believe that a willingness to serve others is a sign of
greatness in God's eyes?

_____

_____

_____

_____

Do I believe that I am surrounded by opportunities
to serve and that I should take advantage of those
opportunities?

_____

_____

_____

_____

SUMMING IT UP

Whether you realize it or not, God has called you
to a life of service. Your job is to find a place
to serve and to get busy.

———◆◆◆◆———

A PRAYER FOR TODAY

Dear Lord, let me help others in every way that I can.
Jesus served others; I can too. I will serve other people
with my good deeds and with my prayers.
And I will give thanks for everybody who helps me.
Amen

Chapter 14

Still Waiting? Maybe It's Time to Be a Little More Reckless

*If you wait for perfect conditions,
you will never get anything done.*

Ecclesiastes 11:4 NLT

THOUGHT OF THE DAY

The habit of procrastination is often rooted in
the fear of failure, the fear of discomfort,
or the fear of embarrassment. Your challenge is to
confront these fears and defeat them.

When something important needs to be done, the best time to do it is sooner rather than later. But sometimes, instead of doing the smart thing (which, by the way, is choosing "sooner"), we may choose "later." When we do, we may pay a heavy price for our shortsightedness.

The habit of procrastination takes a two-fold toll on its victims. First, important work goes unfinished; second (and more importantly), valuable energy is wasted in the process of putting off the things that remain undone. Procrastination results from an individual's short-sighted attempt to postpone temporary discomfort. What results is a senseless cycle of 1. Delay, followed by 2. Worry followed by 3. A panicky and futile attempt to "catch up." Procrastination is, at its core, a struggle against oneself; the only antidote is action.

Once you acquire the habit of doing what needs to be done when it needs to be done, you will avoid untold trouble, worry, and stress. So learn to defeat procrastination by paying less attention to your fears and more attention to your responsibilities.

Are you one of those people who puts things off till the last minute? If so, it's time to change your ways. Whatever "it" is, do it now. When you do, you won't have to worry about "it" later.

MORE IDEAS ABOUT DOING IT NOW

Every time you refuse to face up to life and its problems, you weaken your character.

E. Stanley Jones

Our Lord is searching for people who will make a difference. Christians dare not dissolve into the background or blend into the neutral scenery of the world.

Charles Swindoll

Action springs not from thought, but from a readiness for responsibility.

Dietrich Bonhoeffer

We must not sit still and look for miracles; up and doing, and the Lord will be with thee. Prayer and pains, through faith in Christ Jesus, will do anything.

John Eliot

It is by acts and not by ideas that people live.

Harry Emerson Fosdick

Let us not be content to wait and see what will happen, but give us the determination to make the right things happen.

Peter Marshall

MORE FROM GOD'S WORD

For the Kingdom of God is not just fancy talk; it is living by God's power.

1 Corinthians 4:20 NLT

Therefore, get your minds ready for action, being self-disciplined, and set your hope completely on the grace to be brought to you at the revelation of Jesus Christ.

1 Peter 1:13 HCSB

But prove yourselves doers of the word, and not merely hearers.

James 1:22 NASB

Are there those among you who are truly wise and understanding? Then they should show it by living right and doing good things with a gentleness that comes from wisdom.

James 3:13 NCV

The prudent see danger and take refuge, but the simple keep going and suffer from it.

Proverbs 27:12 NIV

QUESTIONS TO THINK & WRITE ABOUT

Is there an important obligation that I've been putting off? If so, what's a single, specific step I can take that will move me toward the completion of that task?

_____

_____

_____

_____

Is my fear of failure holding me back?

_____

_____

_____

_____

Do I understand the rewards of doing important tasks sooner rather than later?

_____

_____

_____

_____

SUMMING IT UP

The habit of putting things off . . .
is a habit that you're better off without.

A PRAYER FOR TODAY

Dear Lord, even when I'm afraid of failure, give me the
courage to try. Remind me that with You by my side,
I really have nothing to fear. So today, Father,
I will live courageously as I place my faith in You.
Amen

Chapter 15

Whom Shall You Fear?

The Lord is my light and my salvation; whom shall I fear?
The Lord is the strength of my life; of whom shall I be afraid?

Psalm 27:1 NKJV

THOUGHT OF THE DAY

If you are a disciple of the risen Christ, you have every
reason on earth—and in heaven—to live courageously.
Because of your courage, you can be radical, even reckless
at times. And when it comes to taking risks for God,
that's precisely what you should do.

When you form a genuine one-on-one relationship with God, you can be comforted by the fact that wherever you find yourself, whether at the top of the mountain or the depths of the valley, God is there with you. And because your Creator cares for you and protects you, you can live courageously.

God is not a distant being. He is not absent from our world, nor is He absent from your world. God is not "out there;" He is "right here," continuously reshaping His universe, and continuously reshaping the lives of those who dwell in it.

God is with you always, listening to your thoughts and prayers, watching over your every move. If the demands of everyday life weigh down upon you, you may be tempted to ignore God's presence or—worse yet—to lose faith in His promises. But, when you quiet yourself and acknowledge His presence, God will touch your heart and restore your courage.

At this very moment—as you're fulfilling your obligations—God is seeking to work in you and through you. He's asking you to live abundantly and courageously . . . and He's ready to help. So why not let Him do it . . . starting now?

MORE IDEAS ABOUT COURAGE

Why rely on yourself and fall? Cast yourself upon His arm. Be not afraid. He will not let you slip. Cast yourself in confidence. He will receive you and heal you.

St. Augustine

Fill your mind with thoughts of God rather than thoughts of fear.

Norman Vincent Peale

Jesus Christ can make the weakest man into a divine dreadnought, fearing nothing.

Oswald Chambers

Courage faces fear and thereby masters it. Cowardice represses fear and is thereby mastered by it.

Martin Luther King, Jr.

Perhaps I am stronger than I think.

Thomas Merton

Seeing that a Pilot steers the ship in which we sail, who will never allow us to perish even in the midst of shipwrecks, there is no reason why our minds should be overwhelmed with fear and overcome with weariness.

John Calvin

MORE FROM GOD'S WORD

The LORD himself goes before you and will be with you; he will never leave you nor forsake you. Do not be afraid; do not be discouraged.

Deuteronomy 31:8 NIV

So do not fear, for I am with you; do not be dismayed, for I am your God. I will strengthen you and help you; I will uphold you with my righteous right hand.

Isaiah 41:10 NIV

Peace I leave with you, my peace I give unto you: not as the world giveth, give I unto you. Let not your heart be troubled, neither let it be afraid.

John 14:27 KJV

In thee, O Lord, do I put my trust; let me never be put into confusion.

Psalm 71:1 KJV

I can do everything through him that gives me strength.

Philippians 4:13 NIV

QUESTIONS TO THINK & WRITE ABOUT

Do I consider God to be my partner in every aspect of my life?

_____

_____

_____

_____

Do I trust God to handle the problems that are simply too big for me to solve?

_____

_____

_____

_____

Am I really willing to place the future—and my future—in God's hands?

_____

_____

_____

_____

SUMMING IT UP

With God as your partner, you have nothing to fear.
Why? Because you and God, working together,
can handle absolutely anything that comes your way.

———◆◆◆———

A PRAYER FOR TODAY

Lord, I'm only human, and sometimes I am afraid.
But You are always with me, and when I turn to You,
You give me courage. Let me be a courageous,
faith-filled Christian, God, and keep me mindful that,
with You as my protector, I am secure today . . .
and throughout eternity.
Amen

Chapter 16

He Protects You Now and Forever

*Then Moses stretched out his hand over the sea; and the Lord
caused the sea to go back by a strong east wind all that night,
and made the sea into dry land, and the waters were divided.
So the children of Israel went into the midst of the sea
on the dry ground, and the waters were a wall to them
on their right hand and on their left.*

Exodus 14:21-22 NKJV

THOUGHT OF THE DAY

Face it: Earthly security is an illusion. Your only real
security comes from the loving heart of God.

The Old Testament is filled with examples of the surprising methods that God sometimes employs to protect His people. One such story details the parting of the Red Sea. With water ahead and the Pharaoh's army in hot pursuit, it seemed that all was lost for Moses and the children of Israel. But when Moses reached the water's edge, God parted the sea for Moses and his people, demonstrating yet again that God cares for those who are willing to live recklessly in His will.

God protects us, just as He protected Moses. He comforts us in times of adversity. In times of hardship, He restores our strength; in times of sorrow, He dries our tears. When we are troubled or weak or embittered, God is as near as our next breath.

In a world filled with more frustrations than we can count, God's Son offers the ultimate peace. God has promised to protect us, and He intends to fulfill His promise. In a world filled with dangers and temptations, God is the ultimate armor. In a world filled with misleading messages, God's Word is the ultimate truth.

Will you accept God's peace and wear God's armor against the dangers of our world? Hopefully so, because when you do, you can live courageously, knowing that you possess the ultimate protection: God's unfailing love for you.

MORE IDEAS ABOUT GOD'S PROTECTION

There is not only fear, but terrible danger, for the life unguarded by God.

Oswald Chambers

Under heaven's lock and key, we are protected by the most efficient security system available: the power of God.

Charles Swindoll

The promises of God's Word sustain us in our suffering, and we know Jesus sympathizes and empathizes with us in our darkest hour.

Bill Bright

The Rock of Ages is the great sheltering encirclement.

Oswald Chambers

Through all of the crises of life—and we all are going to experience them—we have this magnificent Anchor.

Franklin Graham

There is no safer place to live than the center of His will.

Calvin Miller

MORE FROM GOD'S WORD

Finally, my brethren, be strong in the Lord and in the power of His might. Put on the whole armor of God, that you may be able to stand against the wiles of the devil.

Ephesians 6:10-11 NKJV

The Lord your God in your midst, The Mighty One, will save; He will rejoice over you with gladness, He will quiet you with His love, He will rejoice over you with singing.

Zephaniah 3:17 NKJV

God is my shield, saving those whose hearts are true and right.

Psalm 7:10 NLT

Those who trust the Lord are like Mount Zion, which sits unmoved forever. As the mountains surround Jerusalem, the Lord surrounds his people now and forever.

Psalm 125:1-2 NCV

But the Lord will be a refuge for His people.

Joel 3:16 HCSB

QUESTIONS TO THINK & WRITE ABOUT

Do I believe that God will protect me now and throughout eternity?

_____

_____

_____

_____

Do I trust God's plans even when I cannot understand them?

_____

_____

_____

_____

Am I willing to accept God's unfolding plan for the world—and for my world?

_____

_____

_____

_____

SUMMING IT UP

God wants to protect you and your loved ones.
When you trust your life and your future to God,
He will provide for your needs.

A PRAYER FOR TODAY

Lord, You have promised to protect me, and I will trust
You. Today, I will live courageously as I place my hopes,
my faith, and my life in Your hands. Let my life be
a testimony to the transforming power of Your love,
Your grace, and Your Son.
Amen

Chapter 17

When You Face a Giant Obstacle

*So David prevailed over the Philistine with a sling and a stone,
and struck the Philistine and killed him.
But there was no sword in the hand of David.*

1 Samuel 17:50 NKJV

THOUGHT OF THE DAY

God is in the business of doing miraculous things.
With God as your partner, you can draw from His
strength, and you can accomplish miraculous things.

David didn't just face a giant problem, he faced an actual giant. But instead of focusing on his own inadequacies, David focused on his mighty God. Then, with the assurance that God was on his side, David did the reckless thing: he challenged Goliath . . . and the giant fell.

David tapped into God's strength, and so can you. The Bible promises that you can do great things when you avail yourself of God's power. But how can you tap in? By allowing the Creator to work in you and through you—and by placing Him squarely at the center of your heart, that's how.

Have you really tapped in to God's power? Have you turned your life and your heart over to Him, or are you still trying to do everything by yourself? The answer to these simple questions will determine the quality of your day and the direction of your life.

When you accept God's love and experience His power—when you trust Him to manage His world and yours—you will discover that He offers the strength to live victoriously today, tomorrow, and forever. In times of trouble, He will comfort you; in times of sorrow, He will dry your tears. When you are weak or sorrowful, God is as near as your next breath. He stands at the door of your heart and waits. Welcome Him in and allow Him to rule. And then, accept the peace, the strength, the protection, and the abundance that only God can give.

MORE IDEAS ABOUT GOD'S STRENGTH

Think and care in no way about what is to come. Think more about God and His strength than of yourself and your weakness. If increase of suffering comes, increase of grace will come also.

Gerhard Tersteegen

In leaning upon His Cross, let me not refuse my own; yet in bearing mine, let me bear it by the strength of His.

John Baillie

God's power will liberate us from our weakness and equip us to do His will.

Bill Hybels

We have a God who delights in impossibilities.

Andrew Murray

I have a great need for Christ; I have a great Christ for my need.

C. H. Spurgeon

He can accomplish anything He chooses to do. If He ever asks you to do something, He Himself will enable you to do it.

Henry Blackaby

MORE FROM GOD'S WORD

But the Lord is faithful; he will make you strong and guard you from the evil one.

2 Thessalonians 3:3 NLT

I can do all things through Christ which strengtheneth me.

Philippians 4:13 KJV

The Lord is the strength of my life.

Psalm 27:1 KJV

You are the God who works wonders; You revealed Your strength among the peoples.

Psalm 77:14 HCSB

Search for the Lord and for his strength, and keep on searching. Think of the wonderful works he has done, the miracles and the judgments he handed down.

Psalm 105:4-5 NLT

QUESTIONS TO THINK & WRITE ABOUT

Do I gain strength and courage by allowing Christ to dwell in the center of my heart?

_____

_____

_____

_____

Do I gain strength through prayer?

_____

_____

_____

_____

Do I understand the importance of regular exercise and sensible rest?

_____

_____

_____

_____

SUMMING IT UP

If you're feeling fearful or anxious, you must trust
God to solve the problems that are simply
too big for you to solve.

A PRAYER FOR TODAY

Dear Lord, whatever "it" is, You can handle it!
Let me turn to You when I am fearful or worried.
You are my loving Father, and I will always trust You.
Amen

Chapter 18

The Risk of Sharing Your Testimony

But respect Christ as the holy Lord in your hearts.
Always be ready to answer everyone who asks you
to explain about the hope you have.

1 Peter 3:15 NCV

THOUGHT OF THE DAY

Whether you realize it or not, you have a profound
responsibility to tell as many people as you can about
the eternal life that Christ offers to those who believe in
Him. Sometimes, it may seem risky to share your faith,
but share it you must.

Have you made the decision to allow Christ to reign over your heart? If so, you have an important story to tell: yours.

Your personal testimony is profoundly important, but perhaps because of shyness (or because of the fear of being rebuffed), you've been hesitant to share your experiences. If so, you should start paying less attention to your own insecurities and more attention to the message that God wants you to share with the world.

Let's face facts: You live in a world that desperately needs the healing message of Jesus Christ. Every believer, including you, bears responsibility for sharing the Good News. And it is important to remember that you give your testimony through your words and your actions.

As your faith becomes stronger, you will find ways to share your beliefs with your family, with your friends, with your dates, and with the world. And when you do, everybody wins.

Our faith grows by expression.
If we want to keep our faith,
we must share it. We must act.

—

Billy Graham

MORE IDEAS ABOUT YOUR TESTIMONY

Remember, a small light will do a great deal when it is in a very dark place. Put one little tallow candle in the middle of a large hall, and it will give a great deal of light.

D. L. Moody

Although our actions have nothing to do with gaining our own salvation, they might be used by God to save somebody else! What we do really matters, and it can affect the eternities of people we care about.

Bill Hybels

To stand in an uncaring world and say, "See, here is the Christ" is a daring act of courage.

Calvin Miller

We need to talk to God about people, then talk to people about God.

Dieter Zander

If I can love folks the way they are, we have greater chance of winning them to the kingdom.

Dennis Swanberg

MORE FROM GOD'S WORD

But the following night the Lord stood by him and said, "Be of good cheer, Paul; for as you have testified for Me."

Acts 23:11 NKJV

This and this only has been my appointed work: getting this news to those who have never heard of God, and explaining how it works by simple faith and plain truth.

1 Timothy 2:7 MSG

For God has not given us a spirit of fear and timidity, but of power, love, and self-discipline. So you must never be ashamed to tell others about our Lord.

2 Timothy 1:7-8 NLT

But when the Holy Spirit has come upon you, you will receive power and will tell people about me everywhere—in Jerusalem, throughout Judea, in Samaria, and to the ends of the earth.

Acts 1:8 NLT

You are the light of the world. A city that is set on a hill cannot be hidden. Nor do they light a lamp and put it under a basket, but on a lampstand, and it gives light to all who are in the house. Let your light so shine before men, that they may see your good works and glorify your Father in heaven.

Matthew 5:14–16 NKJV

QUESTIONS TO THINK & WRITE ABOUT

Do I believe that it is important to share my testimony?

_____

_____

_____

_____

Do I feel that my actions are as much a part of my testimony as my words?

_____

_____

_____

_____

Do I feel that my testimony has the power to change the world?

_____

_____

_____

_____

SUMMING IT UP

If you have made the decision to allow Christ
to reign over your heart,
you have an important story to tell: yours.

A PRAYER FOR TODAY

Lord, the life that I live and the words that I speak
will tell the world how I feel about You.
Today and every day, let my testimony be worthy of You.
Let my words be sure and true, and let my actions
point others to You.
Amen

Chapter 19

If It Needs to Be Done, Do It Now!

But prove yourselves doers of the word,
and not merely hearers.

James 1:22 NASB

THOUGHT OF THE DAY

When important work needs to be done,
it's tempting to procrastinate. But God's Word teaches
us to be "doers of the Word," which means taking action
even when we might prefer to do nothing.

The old saying is both familiar and true: actions speak louder than words. And as believers, we must beware: our actions should always give credence to the changes that Christ can make in the lives of those who walk with Him. Doing God's work is a responsibility that each of us must bear, and when we do, our loving Heavenly Father rewards our efforts with a bountiful harvest.

Chronic procrastinators unintentionally squeeze the joy out of their own lives and the lives of their loved ones. So your job is to summon the determination, the wisdom, and the courage (bordering on recklessness) to defeat Old Man Procrastination whenever he arrives at your doorstep.

You can free yourself from the emotional quicksand by paying less attention to your fears and more attention to your responsibilities. So, when you're faced with a difficult choice or an unpleasant responsibility, don't spend endless hours fretting over your fate. Simply seek God's counsel and get busy. When you do, you will be richly rewarded because of your willingness to act.

MORE IDEAS ABOUT DOING IT NOW

It is by acts and not by ideas that people live.

Harry Emerson Fosdick

Our Lord is searching for people who will make a difference. Christians dare not dissolve into the background or blend into the neutral scenery of the world.

Charles Swindoll

God built the body to move.

Dr. Ben Lerner

People create success in their lives by focusing on today. It may sound trite, but today is the only time you have. It's too late for yesterday. And you can't depend on tomorrow.

John Maxwell

Only a person who dares to risk is free.

Joey Johnson

Risk must be taken because the greatest hazard in life is to risk nothing.

John Maxwell

MORE FROM GOD'S WORD

For the Kingdom of God is not just fancy talk; it is living by God's power.

1 Corinthians 4:20 NLT

Therefore, get your minds ready for action, being self-disciplined, and set your hope completely on the grace to be brought to you at the revelation of Jesus Christ.

1 Peter 1:13 HCSB

Are there those among you who are truly wise and understanding? Then they should show it by living right and doing good things with a gentleness that comes from wisdom.

James 3:13 NCV

The prudent see danger and take refuge, but the simple keep going and suffer from it.

Proverbs 27:12 NIV

Do not be lazy but work hard, serving the Lord with all your heart.

Romans 12:11 NCV

QUESTIONS TO THINK & WRITE ABOUT

When I have work that needs to be done, do I usually try to finish the work as soon as possible, or do I put it off?

_____

_____

_____

_____

Do I believe that my testimony is more powerful when actions accompany my words?

_____

_____

_____

_____

Do I see the hypocrisy in saying one thing and doing another, and do I try my best to act in accordance with my beliefs?

_____

_____

_____

_____

SUMMING IT UP

When the time for action arrives, act.
Procrastination is the enemy of progress;
don't let it defeat you.

A PRAYER FOR TODAY

Lord, help me to make choices that are pleasing to You.
Help me to be honest, patient, and kind.
And above all, help me to follow the teachings of Jesus,
not just today, but every day.
Amen

Chapter 20

Making the Most of Your Talents

So he who had received five talents came and brought five other talents, saying, "Lord, you delivered to me five talents; look, I have gained five more talents besides them." His lord said to him, "Well done, good and faithful servant; you were faithful over a few things, I will make you ruler over many things. Enter into the joy of your lord."

Matthew 25:20-21 NKJV

THOUGHT OF THE DAY

God wants His believers to take risks for the kingdom's sake, and He blesses those that do. And He wants all His children (including you) to use the talents He has given them.

God knew precisely what He was doing when He gave you a unique set of talents and opportunities. And now, God wants you to use those talents for the glory of His kingdom. So here's the big question: will you choose to use those talents, or not?

Your Heavenly Father wants you to be a faithful steward of the gifts He has given you. But you live in a society that may encourage you to do otherwise. You face countless temptations to squander your time, your resources, and your talents. So you must be keenly aware of the inevitable distractions that can waste your time, your energy, and your opportunities.

Every day of your life, you have a choice to make: to nurture your talents or to neglect them. When you choose wisely, God rewards your efforts, and He expands your opportunities to serve Him.

God has blessed you with unique opportunities to serve Him, and He has given you every tool that you need to do so. Today, accept this challenge: value the talent that God has given you, nourish it, make it grow, and share it with the world. After all, the best way to say "Thank You" for God's gifts is to use them.

MORE IDEAS ABOUT YOUR TALENTS

You are the only person on earth who can use your ability.

Zig Ziglar

If you want to reach your potential, you need to add a strong work ethic to your talent.

John Maxwell

God often reveals His direction for our lives through the way He made us . . . with a certain personality and unique skills.

Bill Hybels

In the great orchestra we call life, you have an instrument and a song, and you owe it to God to play them both sublimely.

Max Lucado

One thing taught large in the Holy Scriptures is that while God gives His gifts freely, He will require a strict accounting of them at the end of the road. Each man is personally responsible for his store, be it large or small, and will be required to explain his use of it before the judgment seat of Christ.

A. W. Tozer

MORE FROM GOD'S WORD

Do not neglect the gift that is in you.

1 Timothy 4:14 HCSB

Each one has his own gift from God, one in this manner and another in that.

1 Corinthians 7:7 NKJV

I remind you to keep ablaze the gift of God that is in you.

2 Timothy 1:6 HCSB

According to the grace given to us, we have different gifts: If prophecy, use it according to the standard of faith; if service, in service; if teaching, in teaching; if exhorting, in exhortation; giving, with generosity; leading, with diligence; showing mercy, with cheerfulness.

Romans 12:6-8 HCSB

Whatever you do, do it enthusiastically, as something done for the Lord and not for men.

Colossians 3:23 HCSB

QUESTIONS TO THINK & WRITE ABOUT

Am I making the most of my talents?

_____

_____

_____

_____

Am I willing to take sensible risks in the pursuit of spiritual and personal growth?

_____

_____

_____

_____

Is the fear of failure holding me back?

_____

_____

_____

_____

SUMMING IT UP

You are the sole owner of your own set of talents and opportunities. God has given you your own particular gifts—the rest is up to you.

A PRAYER FOR TODAY

Lord, thank You for the talents You have given me. Let me treasure them and use them for Your glory as I walk in the footsteps of Your Son.
Amen

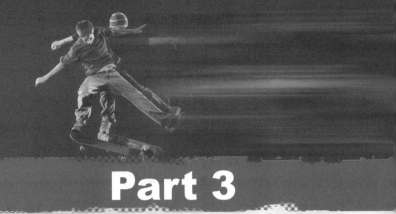

Part 3

RELENTLESS

Chapter 21

Knowing When Not to Quit

*Therefore, my dear brothers, be steadfast, immovable,
always abounding in the Lord's work,
knowing that your labor in the Lord is not in vain.*

1 Corinthians 15:58 HCSB

THOUGHT OF THE DAY

Life is, at times, difficult. When you are tested,
call upon God. He can give you the strength to persevere,
and that's exactly what you should ask Him to do.

Are you one of those people who doesn't give up easily, or are you quick to bail out when the going gets tough? If you've developed the unfortunate habit of giving up at the first sign of trouble, it's probably time for you to have a heart-to-heart talk with the guy you see every time you look in the mirror.

A well-lived life is like a marathon, not a sprint—it calls for preparation, determination, and lots of perseverance. As an example of perfect perseverance, you need look no further than your Savior, Jesus Christ.

Jesus finished what He began, and so should you. Christ was unwavering in His faithfulness to God. You, too, should remain faithful, especially when times are tough.

Are you facing a difficult situation? If so, remember this: whatever your problem, God can handle it. Your job is to keep persevering until He does.

By perseverance
the snail reached the ark.

—

C. H. Spurgeon

MORE IDEAS ABOUT THE POWER OF PERSEVERANCE

That is the source of Jeremiah's living persistence, his creative constancy. He was up before the sun, listening to God's word. Rising early, he was quiet and attentive before his Lord. Long before the yelling started, the mocking, the complaining, there was this centering, discovering, exploring time with God.

Eugene Peterson

Battles are won in the trenches, in the grit and grime of courageous determination; they are won day by day in the arena of life.

Charles Swindoll

Only the man who follows the command of Jesus single-mindedly and unresistingly lets his yoke rest upon him, finds his burden easy, and under its gentle pressure receives the power to persevere in the right way.

Dietrich Bonhoeffer

I learned as never before that persistent calling upon the Lord breaks through every stronghold of the devil, for nothing is impossible with God. For Christians in these troubled times, there is simply no other way.

Jim Cymbala

In all negotiations of difficulties, a man may not look to sow and reap at once. He must prepare his business and so ripen it by degrees.

Francis Bacon

Press on. Obstacles are seldom the same size tomorrow as they are today.

Robert Schuller

Keep adding, keep walking, keep advancing; do not stop, do not turn back, do not turn from the straight road.

St. Augustine

Perseverance is more than endurance. It is endurance combined with absolute assurance and certainty that what we are looking for is going to happen.

Oswald Chambers

The value of good work depends on perseverance. You live a good life in vain if you do not continue it until you die.

St. Gregory

In the Bible, patience is not a passive acceptance of circumstances. It is a courageous perseverance in the face of suffering and difficulty.

Warren Wiersbe

MORE FROM GOD'S WORD

But as for you, be strong; don't be discouraged, for your work has a reward.

2 Chronicles 15:7 HCSB

I have fought the good fight, I have finished the race, I have kept the faith.

2 Timothy 4:7 HCSB

So we must not get tired of doing good, for we will reap at the proper time if we don't give up.

Galatians 6:9 HCSB

Let us lay aside every weight and the sin that so easily ensnares us, and run with endurance the race that lies before us, keeping our eyes on Jesus, the source and perfecter of our faith.

Hebrews 12:1-2 HCSB

Now we want each of you to demonstrate the same diligence for the final realization of your hope, so that you won't become lazy, but imitators of those who inherit the promises through faith and perseverance.

Hebrews 6:11-12 HCSB

QUESTIONS TO THINK & WRITE ABOUT

Do I have a healthy respect for the power of perseverance?

_____

_____

_____

_____

Do I ask God to give me strength every day?

_____

_____

_____

_____

Do I associate with people who encourage me to be courageous, optimistic, energetic, and persistent?

_____

_____

_____

_____

SUMMING IT UP

If things don't work out at first, don't quit.
If you never try, you'll never know how good you can be.

A PRAYER FOR TODAY

Lord, some days I feel like there's no way I can win.
But when I'm discouraged, let me turn to You for
strength, courage, and faith. When I find my strength in
You, Lord, I am protected, today and forever.
Amen

Chapter 22

Fully Grown?

So let us stop going over the basics of Christianity again and again. Let us go on instead and become mature in our understanding.

Hebrews 6:1 NLT

THOUGHT OF THE DAY

When it comes to your faith, God doesn't intend for you to stand still. He wants you to be relentless in the pursuit of spiritual growth. God wants you to keep moving and growing.

When it comes to your faith, God doesn't intend for you to stand still. He wants you to keep moving and growing. In fact, God's plan for you includes a lifetime of prayer, praise, and spiritual growth.

When will you be a "fully-grown" Christian? Hopefully never—or at least not until you arrive in heaven! As a believer living here on planet earth, you're never "fully grown"; you always have the potential to keep growing.

Would you like a time-tested formula for spiritual growth? Here it is: keep studying God's Word, keep obeying His commandments, keep praying (and listening for answers), and keep trying to live in the center of God's will. And while you're at it, find friends who encourage you to grow. When you do these things, you'll never stay stuck for long. You will, instead, be a growing Christian . . . and that's precisely the kind of Christian God wants you to be.

When you're through changing, you're through!

—

John Maxwell

MORE IDEAS ABOUT SPIRITUAL GROWTH

God loves us the way we are, but He loves us too much to leave us that way.

Leighton Ford

Spiritual growth consists most in the growth of the root, which is out of sight.

Matthew Henry

Salvation is the process that's done, that's secure, that no one can take away from you. Sanctification is the lifelong process of being changed from one degree of glory to the next, growing in Christ, putting away the old, taking on the new.

Max Lucado

When I was young I was sure of everything; in a few years, having been mistaken a thousand times, I was not half so sure of most things as I was before; at present, I am hardly sure of anything but what God has revealed to me.

John Wesley

We are not yet what we should be, what we can be, or what we will be when we see the Lord.

John MacArthur

MORE FROM GOD'S WORD

For this reason we also, since the day we heard it, do not cease to pray for you, and to ask that you may be filled with the knowledge of His will in all wisdom and spiritual understanding.

Colossians 1:9 NKJV

Watch the way you talk. Let nothing foul or dirty come out of your mouth. Say only what helps, each word a gift.

Ephesians 4:29 MSG

But grow in the grace and knowledge of our Lord and Savior Jesus Christ. To Him be the glory both now and to the day of eternity.

2 Peter 3:18 HCSB

I want their hearts to be encouraged and joined together in love, so that they may have all the riches of assured understanding, and have the knowledge of God's mystery—Christ.

Colossians 2:2 HCSB

For You, O God, have tested us; You have refined us as silver is refined. You brought us into the net; You laid affliction on our backs. You have caused men to ride over our heads; we went through fire and through water; but You brought us out to rich fulfillment.

Psalm 66:10–12 NKJV

QUESTIONS TO THINK & WRITE ABOUT

Do I believe that the level of my spiritual maturity has a direct impact, either positively or negatively, on those around me?

_____

_____

_____

_____

Do I believe that I still have "room to grow" in my faith?

_____

_____

_____

_____

Do I believe that spiritual growth usually happens day by day, and do I try to keep growing every day?

_____

_____

_____

_____

SUMMING IT UP

Spiritual maturity is a journey, not a destination—
and a growing relationship with God
should be your highest priority.

A PRAYER FOR TODAY

Dear Lord, the Bible tells me that You are at work
in my life, continuing to help me grow and to mature
in my faith. Show me Your wisdom, Father,
and let me live according to Your Word and Your will.
Amen

Chapter 23

God's Timetable

Wait patiently on the Lord. Be brave and courageous.
Yes, wait patiently on the Lord.

Psalm 27:14 NLT

THOUGHT OF THE DAY

You have a timetable, and God has a timetable.
His is better than yours.

For most of us, patience is a hard thing to master. Why? Because we have lots of things we want, and we know precisely when we want them: NOW (if not sooner). But our Father in heaven has other ideas; the Bible teaches that we must learn to wait patiently for the things that God has in store for us, even when waiting is difficult.

Are you a guy in a hurry? If so, you may be in for a few disappointments. Why? Because life has a way of unfolding according to its own timetable, not yours. That's why life requires patience . . . and lots of it!

Lamentations 3:25 reminds us that, "The Lord is wonderfully good to those who wait for him and seek him" (NIV). But, for most of us, waiting quietly is difficult because we're in such a hurry for things to happen!

The next time you find your patience tested to the limit, slow down, take a deep breath, and relax. Sometimes life can't be hurried—and during those times, patience is indeed a priceless virtue.

MORE IDEAS ABOUT PATIENCE

You can't step in front of God and not get in trouble. When He says, "Go three steps," don't go four.

Charles Stanley

In all negotiations of difficulties, a man may not look to sow and reap at once. He must prepare his business and so ripen it by degrees.

Francis Bacon

As we wait on God, He helps us use the winds of adversity to soar above our problems. As the Bible says, "Those who wait on the LORD . . . shall mount up with wings like eagles."

Billy Graham

God never hurries. There are no deadlines against which He must work. To know this is to quiet our spirits and relax our nerves.

A. W. Tozer

God is in no hurry. Compared to the works of mankind, He is extremely deliberate. God is not a slave to the human clock.

Charles Swindoll

MORE FROM GOD'S WORD

Knowing God leads to self-control. Self-control leads to patient endurance, and patient endurance leads to godliness.

2 Peter 1:6 NLT

Now we exhort you, brethren, warn those who are unruly, comfort the fainthearted, uphold the weak, be patient with all.

1 Thessalonians 5:14 NKJV

Patience of spirit is better than haughtiness of spirit.

Ecclesiastes 7:8 NASB

God has chosen you and made you his holy people. He loves you. So always do these things: Show mercy to others, be kind, humble, gentle, and patient.

Colossians 3:12 NCV

And the servant of the Lord must not strive; but be gentle unto all men, apt to teach, patient; in meekness instructing those that oppose themselves . . . .

2 Timothy 2:24-25 KJV

QUESTIONS TO THINK & WRITE ABOUT

Do I take seriously the Bible's instructions to be patient?

_____

_____

_____

_____

Do I believe that patience is not idle waiting but that it is an activity that means watching and waiting for God to lead me in the direction of His choosing?

_____

_____

_____

_____

Even when I don't understand the circumstances that confront me, do I strive to wait patiently while serving the Lord?

_____

_____

_____

_____

SUMMING IT UP

Remember that God's timing is best.
So don't allow yourself to become discouraged if things
don't work out exactly as you wish. Instead of worrying
about your future, entrust it to God. He knows exactly
what you need and exactly when you need it.

———◆◆◆◆◆———

A PRAYER FOR TODAY

Lord, sometimes I can be a very impatient person.
Slow me down and calm me down. Let me trust in
Your plan, Father; let me trust in Your timetable;
and let me trust in Your love for me.
Amen

Chapter 24

Never Lose Hope

*Let us hold fast the confession of our hope without wavering,
for He who promised is faithful.*

Hebrews 10:23 NASB

THOUGHT OF THE DAY

Since God has promised to guide and protect you—
now and forever—you should never lose hope.

There are few sadder sights on earth than the sight of a guy who has lost hope. In difficult times, hope can be elusive, but those who place their faith in God's promises need never lose it. After all, God is good; His love endures; He has promised His children the gift of eternal life. And, God keeps His promises.

Despite God's promises, despite Christ's love, and despite our countless blessings, we're only human, and we can still lose hope from time to time. When we do, we need the encouragement of Christian friends, the life-changing power of prayer, and the healing truth of God's Holy Word.

If you find yourself falling into the spiritual traps of worry and discouragement, seek the healing touch of Jesus and the encouraging words of fellow believers. And if you find a friend in need, remind him or her of the peace that is found through a genuine relationship with Christ. It was Christ who promised, "I have told you these things so that in Me you may have peace. In the world you have suffering. But take courage! I have conquered the world" (John 16:33 HCSB). This world can be a place of trials and troubles, but as believers, we are secure. God has promised us peace, joy, and eternal life. And, of course, God keeps His promises today, tomorrow, and forever.

Faith looks back
and draws courage;
hope looks ahead
and keeps desire alive.

—

John Eldredge

MORE IDEAS ABOUT HOPE

Hope is nothing more than the expectation of those things which faith has believed to be truly promised by God.

John Calvin

I wish I could make it all new again; I can't. But God can. "He restores my soul," wrote the shepherd. God doesn't reform; he restores. He doesn't camouflage the old; he restores the new. The Master Builder will pull out the original plan and restore it. He will restore the vigor, he will restore the energy. He will restore the hope. He will restore the soul.

Max Lucado

There is wisdom in the habit of looking at the bright side of life.

Father Flanagan

Oh, remember this: There is never a time when we may not hope in God. Whatever our necessities, however great our difficulties, and though to all appearance help is impossible, yet our business is to hope in God, and it will be found that it is not in vain.

George Mueller

Great hopes make great men.

Thomas Fuller

Christ has turned all our sunsets into dawn.

St. Clement of Alexandria

People are genuinely motivated by hope and a part of that hope is the assurance of future glory with God for those who are His people.

Warren Wiersbe

Nothing worth doing is completed in our lifetimes, therefore we must be saved by hope.

Reinhold Niebuhr

The popular idea of faith is of a certain obstinate optimism: the hope, tenaciously held in the face of trouble, that the universe is fundamentally friendly and things may get better.

J. I. Packer

The hope we have in Jesus is the anchor for the soul— something sure and steadfast, preventing drifting or giving way, lowered to the depth of God's love.

Franklin Graham

MORE FROM GOD'S WORD

The lines of purpose in your lives never grow slack, tightly tied as they are to your future in heaven, kept taut by hope.

Colossians 1:5 MSG

I wait for the Lord, my soul waits, And in His word I do hope. My soul waits for the Lord More than those who watch for the morning—Yes, more than those who watch for the morning.

Psalm 130:5-6 NKJV

Now faith is the substance of things hoped for, the evidence of things not seen.

Hebrews 11:1 KJV

This hope we have as an anchor of the soul, a hope both sure and steadfast.

Hebrews 6:19 NASB

Full of hope, you'll relax, confident again; you'll look around, sit back, and take it easy.

Job 11:18 MSG

QUESTIONS TO THINK & WRITE ABOUT

Do I believe that genuine hope begins with hope in a sovereign God?

_____

_____

_____

_____

Am I confident in God's promise to protect me now and throughout all eternity?

_____

_____

_____

_____

Do I really believe that God offers me "a peace that passes understanding," and do I really desire to accept God's peace?

_____

_____

_____

_____

SUMMING IT UP

If you're experiencing hard times, you'll be wise
to start spending more time with God.
And if you do your part, God will do His part.
So never be afraid to hope—or to ask—for a miracle.

A PRAYER FOR TODAY

Dear Lord, I will place my hope in You. If I become
discouraged, I will turn to You. If I am afraid,
I will seek strength in You. In every aspect of my life,
I will trust You. You are my Father, and I will place my
hope, my trust, and my faith in You.
Amen

Chapter 25

Beyond Worry

Cast your burden upon the Lord and He will sustain you:
He will never allow the righteous to be shaken.

Psalm 55:22 NASB

THOUGHT OF THE DAY

You have worries, but God has solutions.
Your challenge is to trust Him
to solve the problems that you can't.

A re you willing to guard your heart against worry? Well, that's what the Bible says you should do.

When you're worried, there are two places you should take your concerns: to the people who love you and to God. When troubles arise (as they will from time to time), it helps to talk things over with parents, grandparents, concerned adults, and trusted friends. But you shouldn't stop there: you should also have a heart-to-heart talk with God.

If you're worried about something, pray about it. Remember that God is always listening, and He always wants to hear from you.

So when you're upset about your life or your future, try this simple plan: talk and pray. Talk openly to the people who love you, and pray to the Heavenly Father who made you. The more you talk and the more you pray, the better you'll feel.

MORE IDEAS ABOUT WORRY

We know so little about the future that to worry about it would be the height of foolishness.

C. H. Spurgeon

The beginning of anxiety is the end of faith, and the beginning of true faith is the end of anxiety.

George Mueller

Pray, and let God worry.

Martin Luther

Today is the tomorrow we worried about yesterday.

Dennis Swanberg

Worry and anxiety are sand in the machinery of life; faith is the oil.

E. Stanley Jones

God is bigger than your problems. Whatever worries press upon you today, put them in God's hands and leave them there.

Billy Graham

MORE FROM GOD'S WORD

Don't worry about anything, but in everything, through prayer and petition with thanksgiving, let your requests be made known to God.

Philippians 4:6 HCSB

I will be with you when you pass through the waters . . . when you walk through the fire . . . the flame will not burn you. For I the Lord your God, the Holy One of Israel, and your Savior.

Isaiah 43:2-3 HCSB

Your heart must not be troubled. Believe in God; believe also in Me.

John 14:1 HCSB

Come to Me, all you who labor and are heavy laden, and I will give you rest. Take My yoke upon you and learn from Me, for I am gentle and lowly in heart, and you will find rest for your souls. For My yoke is easy and My burden is light.

Matthew 11:28-30 NKJV

Those who trust in the Lord are like Mount Zion. It cannot be shaken; it remains forever.

Psalm 125:1 HCSB

QUESTIONS TO THINK & WRITE ABOUT

Am I willing to trust God in every season of life, in good times and hard times?

_____

_____

_____

_____

Do I use faith as an antidote to worry?

_____

_____

_____

_____

Am I willing to trust God's Word, and do I expect Him to fulfill His promises?

_____

_____

_____

_____

SUMMING IT UP

Work hard, pray harder, and if you have any worries,
take them to God—and leave them there.

A PRAYER FOR TODAY

Lord, sometimes, I can't seem to help myself;
I worry. Even though I know to put my trust in You,
I still become anxious about the future. Give me
the wisdom to trust in You, Father, and give me
the courage to live a life of faith, not a life of fear.
Amen

Chapter 26

Finding Strength in All the Right Places

And He said to me, "My grace is sufficient for you, for My strength is made perfect in weakness."

2 Corinthians 12:9 NKJV

THOUGHT OF THE DAY

When you are tired, fearful, or discouraged, God can restore your strength. Your job is to ask Him.

Where do you go to find strength? The gym? The health food store? The espresso bar? There's a better source of strength, of course, and that source is God. He is a never-ending source of strength and courage if you call upon Him.

Are you an energized Christian? You should be. But if you're not, you must seek strength and renewal from the source that will never fail: that source, of course, is your Heavenly Father. And rest assured—when you sincerely petition Him, He will give you all the strength you need to live victoriously for Him.

The Bible tells us that we can do all things through the power of our risen Savior, Jesus Christ. But what does the Bible say about our powers outside the will of Christ? The Bible teaches us that "the wages of sin is death" (Romans 6:23). Our challenge, then, is clear: we must place Christ where He belongs: at the very center of our lives. When we do so, we will surely discover that He offers us the strength to live victoriously in this world and eternally in the next.

So today, it's time to turn your concerns and your prayers over to God. He knows your needs, and He has promised to meet those needs. Whatever your circumstances, God will protect you and care for you . . . if you let Him. Invite Him into your heart and allow Him to renew your spirits. When you trust Him and Him alone, He will never fail you.

MORE IDEAS ABOUT STRENGTH

God gives us always strength enough, and sense enough, for everything he wants us to do.

John Ruskin

If you are weak, limited, ordinary, you are the best material through which God can work!

Henry Blackaby and Claude King

God is the One who provides our strength, not only to cope with the demands of the day, but also to rise above them. May we look to Him for the strength to soar.

Jim Gallery

Jesus is not a strong man making men and women who gather around Him weak. He is the Strong creating the strong.

E. Stanley Jones

What is it that keeps me and you close to God in the good times? It is in solitude, quietness, waiting, and listening. It is seeking before anything and everything the face and the voice of God.

Ronald E. Wilson

MORE FROM GOD'S WORD

Be strong! We must prove ourselves strong for our people and for the cities of our God. May the Lord's will be done.

1 Chronicles 19:13 HCSB

And He said to me, "My grace is sufficient for you, for My strength is made perfect in weakness."

2 Corinthians 12:9 NKJV

Finally, be strengthened by the Lord and by His vast strength.

Ephesians 6:10 HCSB

The LORD is my strength and my song . . . .

Exodus 15:2 NIV

Those who hope in the LORD will renew their strength. They will soar on wings like eagles; they will run and not grow weary, they will walk and not be faint.

Isaiah 40:31 NIV

QUESTIONS TO THINK & WRITE ABOUT

When I am tired or discouraged, do I turn to God for strength?

_____

_____

_____

_____

Do I gain strength each morning through prayer and Bible study?

_____

_____

_____

_____

When I've done my best, can I entrust the outcome to God, or do I continue to worry?

_____

_____

_____

_____

SUMMING IT UP

When in doubt, turn your worries and your struggles
over to God. He can handle them . . . and will.

A PRAYER FOR TODAY

Dear Lord, let me turn to You for strength.
When I am weak, You lift me up. When my spirit
is crushed, You comfort me. When I am victorious,
Your Word reminds me to be humble.
Today and every day, I will turn to You,
Father, for strength, for hope,
for wisdom, and for salvation.
Amen

Chapter 27

Relentless Forgiveness

*Then Peter came to Him and said, "Lord, how many times
could my brother sin against me and I forgive him?
As many as seven times?" "I tell you, not as many as seven,"
Jesus said to him, "but 70 times seven."*

Matthew 18:21-22 HCSB

THOUGHT OF THE DAY

When it comes to the task of forgiving others,
God wants you to be relentless. He wants you to start
forgiving now and keep forgiving until it sticks.

Forgiving other people is hard—sometimes very hard. But God tells us that we must forgive others, even when we'd rather not. So, if you're angry with anybody (or if you're upset by something you yourself have done), it's time to forgive . . . now!

Life would be much simpler if you could forgive people "once and for all" and be done with it. Yet forgiveness is seldom that easy. Usually, the decision to forgive is straightforward, but the process of forgiving is more difficult. Forgiveness is a journey that requires effort, time, perseverance, and prayer.

God instructs you to treat other people exactly as you wish to be treated. And since you want to be forgiven for the mistakes that you make, you must be willing to extend forgiveness to other people for the mistakes that they have made. If you can't seem to forgive someone, you should keep asking God to help you until you do. And you can be sure of this: if you keep asking for God's help, He will give it.

MORE IDEAS ABOUT FORGIVENESS

Only the truly forgiven are truly forgiving.

C. S. Lewis

He who is filled with love is filled with God Himself.

St. Augustine

As you have received the mercy of God by the forgiveness of sin and the promise of eternal life, thus you must show mercy.

Billy Graham

To hold on to hate and resentments is to throw a monkey wrench into the machinery of life.

E. Stanley Jones

Revenge is the raging fire that consumes the arsonist.

Max Lucado

By not forgiving, by not letting wrongs go, we aren't getting back at anyone. We are merely punishing ourselves by barricading our own hearts.

Jim Cymbala

MORE FROM GOD'S WORD

And whenever you stand praying, if you have anything against anyone, forgive him, so that your Father in heaven may also forgive you your wrongdoing.

Mark 11:25 HCSB

And be ye kind one to another, tenderhearted, forgiving one another, even as God for Christ's sake hath forgiven you.

Ephesians 4:32 KJV

Be even-tempered, content with second place, quick to forgive an offense. Forgive as quickly and completely as the Master forgave you. And regardless of what else you put on, wear love. It's your basic, all-purpose garment. Never be without it.

Colossians 3:13-14 MSG

Hatred stirs up trouble, but love forgives all wrongs.

Proverbs 10:12 NCV

Blessed are the merciful, because they will be shown mercy.

Matthew 5:7 HCSB

QUESTIONS TO THINK & WRITE ABOUT

Am I willing to acknowledge the important role that forgiveness should play in my life?

_____

_____

_____

_____

Will I strive to forgive those who have hurt me, even when doing so is difficult?

_____

_____

_____

_____

Do I understand that forgiveness is a marathon (not a sprint), and will I prayerfully ask God to help me move beyond the emotions of bitterness and regret?

_____

_____

_____

_____

SUMMING IT UP

Forgiveness is its own reward.
Bitterness is its own punishment.
Guard your words and your thoughts accordingly.

A PRAYER FOR TODAY

Lord, just as You have forgiven me, I am going to forgive
others. When I forgive others, I not only obey
Your commandments, but I also free myself from
bitterness and regret. Forgiveness is Your way, Lord,
and I will make it my way, too. Amen

Chapter 28

Persistence Precedes Success

Blessed is the man who perseveres under trial, because when he has stood the test, he will receive the crown of life that God has promised to those who love him.

James 1:12 NIV

THOUGHT OF THE DAY

Success seldom comes easily. Usually, it takes perseverance, and lots of it, to achieve your goals— and to accomplish God's plan—for your life.

Wouldn't it be nice if we could uncover a few "secrets" to success? But we can't. Why? Because the keys to a successful life aren't really secrets at all—the keys to success are simply those good, old-fashioned, common-sense principles that we've heard since we were children. And the good news is this: those principles really do work.

Do you want to be successful? Then here are four things you should do:

1. Put God First: When you do, all your other priorities will begin to fall into place.

2. Be Relentless and Be Patient: If you give up at the first sign of trouble, you'll never know how good you might have been.

3. When You Find Yourself at the End of a Dead-end Street, Turn Around: If you need to change directions, it's better to change sooner rather than later.

4. Be Careful How You Define Success: Genuine success has little to do with fame or fortune; it has everything to do with God's gift of love and His promise of salvation.

If you have accepted Christ as your personal Savior, you are already a towering success in the eyes of God, but there is still more that you can do. Your task—as a believer who has been touched by the Creator's grace—is to accept the spiritual abundance and peace that He offers through the person of His Son. Then, you can share the healing message of God's love and His abundance with a world that desperately needs both. When you do, you will have reached the pinnacle of success.

MORE IDEAS ABOUT PERSISTENCE

Don't quit. For if you do, you may miss the answer to your prayers.

Max Lucado

Untold damage has been done to the cause of Christ because some people gear up for a sprint when they need to train for the marathon.

Bill Hybels

Let us not cease to do the utmost, that we may incessantly go forward in the way of the Lord; and let us not despair of the smallness of our accomplishments.

John Calvin

When our hopes break, let our patience hold.

Thomas Fuller

Jesus taught that perseverance is the essential element in prayer.

E. M. Bounds

MORE FROM GOD'S WORD

Do not fear, for I am with you; do not be afraid, for I am your God. I will strengthen you; I will help you; I will hold on to you with My righteous right hand.

Isaiah 41:10 HCSB

There's no telling who will hate you because of me. Even so, every detail of your body and soul—even the hairs of your head!—is in my care; nothing of you will be lost. Staying with it—that's what is required. Stay with it to the end. You won't be sorry; you'll be saved.

Luke 21:17-19 MSG

What a gift life is to those who stay the course! You've heard, of course, of Job's staying power, and you know how God brought it all together for him at the end. That's because God cares, cares right down to the last detail.

James 5:11 MSG

Brothers, I do not consider myself to have taken hold of it. But one thing I do: forgetting what is behind and reaching forward to what is ahead, I pursue as my goal the prize promised by God's heavenly call in Christ Jesus.

Philippians 3:13-14 HCSB

QUESTIONS TO THINK & WRITE ABOUT

Do I have a healthy respect for the power of persistence?

_____

_____

_____

_____

When I am discouraged, do I turn to God for strength?

_____

_____

_____

_____

Am I searching for success according to God, or am I allowing society to dictate my definition of success?

_____

_____

_____

_____

SUMMING IT UP

Success according to God requires perseverance,
prayer, and patience—if you want to be successful,
you'll need all three.

A PRAYER FOR TODAY

Dear Lord, life is not a sprint, but a marathon.
When the pace of my life becomes frantic, slow me down
and give me perspective. Keep me steady and sure.
When I become weary, let me persevere so that,
in Your time, I might finish my work here on earth,
and that You might then say,
"Well done my good and faithful servant."
Amen

Chapter 29

Renewing Your Strength

I will give you a new heart and put a new spirit within you.
Ezekiel 36:26 HCSB

THOUGHT OF THE DAY

God can make all things new, including you.
When you are weak or worried,
God can restore your spirit. Your task is to let Him.

E ven the most inspired Christian guys can find themselves running on empty. Even the most well-intentioned guys can run out of energy; even the most hopeful believers can be burdened by fears and doubts. And you are no exception.

When you're exhausted or worried—or worse—there is a source from which you can draw the power needed to recharge your spiritual batteries. That source is God.

God intends that His children lead joyous lives filled with abundance and peace. But sometimes, abundance and peace seem very far away. During these difficult days, we must turn to God for renewal, and when we do, He will restore us.

Are you tired or troubled? Turn your heart toward God in prayer. Are you weak or worried? Take the time—or, more accurately, make the time—to delve deeply into God's Holy Word. Are you spiritually depleted? Call upon fellow believers to support you, and call upon Christ to renew your spirit and your life. When you do, you'll discover that the Creator of the universe stands always ready and always able to create a new sense of wonderment and joy in you.

MORE IDEAS ABOUT RENEWING YOUR FAITH AND YOUR STRENGTH

The same voice that brought Lazarus out of the tomb raised us to newness of life.

C. H. Spurgeon

Walking with God leads to receiving his intimate counsel, and counseling leads to deep restoration.

John Eldredge

God is not running an antique shop! He is making all things new!

Vance Havner

No matter how badly we have failed, we can always get up and begin again. Our God is the God of new beginnings.

Warren Wiersbe

Father, for this day, renew within me the gift of the Holy Spirit.

Andrew Murray

Troubles we bear trustfully can bring us a fresh vision of God and a new outlook on life, an outlook of peace and hope.

Billy Graham

MORE FROM GOD'S WORD

But may the God of all grace, who called us to His eternal glory by Christ Jesus, after you have suffered a while, perfect, establish, strengthen, and settle you.

1 Peter 5:10 NKJV

Finally, brothers, rejoice. Be restored, be encouraged, be of the same mind, be at peace, and the God of love and peace will be with you.

2 Corinthians 13:11 HCSB

But those who wait on the Lord Shall renew their strength; They shall mount up with wings like eagles, They shall run and not be weary, They shall walk and not faint.

Isaiah 40:31 NKJV

Therefore if anyone is in Christ, he is a new creature; the old things passed away; behold, new things have come.

2 Corinthians 5:17 HCSB

Then the One seated on the throne said, "Look! I am making everything new."

Revelation 21:5 HCSB

QUESTIONS TO THINK & WRITE ABOUT

Do I believe that God can make all things new—including me?

_____

_____

_____

_____

Do I take time each day to be still and let God give me perspective and direction?

_____

_____

_____

_____

Do I understand the importance of getting a good night's sleep?

_____

_____

_____

_____

SUMMING IT UP

God wants to give you peace, and He wants to renew your spirit. It's up to you to slow down and give Him a chance to do so.

A PRAYER FOR TODAY

Lord, You are my rock and my strength.
When I am discouraged, restore my faith in You.
Let me always trust in Your promises, Lord,
and let me draw strength from those promises
and from Your unending love.
Amen

Chapter 30

His Great Commission

"Go therefore and make disciples of all the nations, baptizing them in the name of the Father and of the Son and of the Holy Spirit, teaching them to observe all things that I have commanded you; and lo, I am with you always, even to the end of the age." Amen.

Matthew 28:19-20 NKJV

THOUGHT OF THE DAY

God's Word clearly instructs you to share His Good News with the world. If you're willing, God will empower you to share your faith. So when it comes to the vitally important task of sharing the Gospel, please share it relentlessly.

After His resurrection, Jesus addressed His disciples. As recorded in the 28th chapter of Matthew, Christ instructed His followers to share His message with the world. This "Great Commission" applies to Christians of every generation, including our own.

As believers, we are called to share the Good News of Jesus Christ with our families, with our neighbors, and with the world. Yet many of us are slow to obey the last commandment of the risen Christ; we simply don't do our best to "make disciples of all the nations." Although our personal testimonies are vitally important, we sometimes hesitate to share our experiences. And that's unfortunate.

Billy Graham observed, "Our faith grows by expression. If we want to keep our faith, we must share it." If you are a follower of Christ, the time to express your belief in Him is now.

You know how Jesus has touched your heart; help Him do the same for others. You must do likewise, and you must do so today. Tomorrow may indeed be too late.

MORE IDEAS ABOUT SHARING
THE GOOD NEWS

Missions is God finding those whose hearts are right with Him and placing them where they can make a difference for His kingdom.

Henry Blackaby

The evangelistic harvest is always urgent. The destiny of men and of nations is always being decided. Every generation is strategic. We are not responsible for the past generation, and we cannot bear the full responsibility for the next one, but we do have our generation. God will hold us responsible as to how well we fulfill our responsibilities to this age and take advantage of our opportunities.

Billy Graham

Taking the gospel to people wherever they are—death row, the ghetto, or next door—is frontline evangelism, frontline love. It is our one hope for breaking down barriers and for restoring the sense of community, of caring for one another, that our decadent, impersonalized culture has sucked out of us.

Chuck Colson

MORE FROM GOD'S WORD

But you will receive power when the Holy Spirit has come upon you, and you will be My witnesses in Jerusalem, in all Judea and Samaria, and to the ends of the earth.

Acts 1:8 HCSB

After this the Lord appointed 70 others, and He sent them ahead of Him in pairs to every town and place where He Himself was about to go. He told them: "The harvest is abundant, but the workers are few. Therefore, pray to the Lord of the harvest to send out workers into His harvest. Now go; I'm sending you out like lambs among wolves."

Luke 10:1-3 HCSB

But you will receive power when the Holy Spirit has come upon you, and you will be My witnesses in Jerusalem, in all Judea and Samaria, and to the ends of the earth.

Acts 1:8 HCSB

This good news of the kingdom will be proclaimed in all the world as a testimony to all nations.

Matthew 24:14 HCSB

Now then we are ambassadors for Christ . . . .

2 Corinthians 5:20 KJV

QUESTIONS TO THINK & WRITE ABOUT

Do I genuinely appreciate the importance of sharing God's message with the world?

_____

_____

_____

_____

Do I believe that God will empower me to share my faith?

_____

_____

_____

_____

Am I willing to look for unplanned opportunities to share the Good News of Jesus Christ?

_____

_____

_____

_____

SUMMING IT UP

If you're willing, God will use you to share
His message and care for His children.
When you become willing to share the Good News,
God will guide your steps and bless your endeavors.

A PRAYER FOR TODAY

Heavenly Father, every man and woman, every boy
and girl is Your child. You desire that all Your children
know Jesus as their Lord and Savior. Father, let me be
part of Your Great Commission. Let me give, let me pray,
and let me go out into this world so that
I might be a fisher of men . . . for You.
Amen